THE
MYWAY
CODE

To Kate, Rachel and Filthy MacNasty's

THE
MYWAY
CODE

Dan Kieran & Ian Vince

B🌱XTREE

First published 2006 by Boxtree
an imprint of Pan Macmillan Ltd
Pan Macmillan, 20 New Wharf Road, London N1 9RR
Basingstoke and Oxford
Associated companies throughout the world
www.panmacmillan.com

ISBN-13: 978-0-752-2260-0
ISBN-10: 0-752-22620-7

9 8 7 6 5 4 3 2 1

A CIP catalogue record for this book is available from
the British Library.

Colour reproduction by Aylesbury Studios Ltd, Bromley, Kent
Printed and bound in Great Britain by Butler and Tanner

Contents

The Code

Introduction

Note: You are forbidden to read this book until you have passed your driving test.

Have you passed your driving test?

Congratulations! Now that you have passed your practical driving test you no longer have to suffer the tedious mutterings of your driving instructor, bleating 'Mirror, signal, manoeuvre' in your ear as you attempt a doughnut outside the gates of your old secondary school.

Once obtained, your full driving licence will enable you to throw away your 'ten to two' steering position along with your 'L' plates. Many of the rules you have been taught are legal requirements developed over years of careful governmental study to raise standards and cut back congestion on Britain's roads, but **SOD THAT,** it's time to drive like a man.

About this book

The Myway Code is absolutely essential reading for the country's road users.

As a direct result, motorists, cyclists and airline pilots, as well as horsy people and the scattered organs of crushed mammals, are all subject to its all-knowing wisdom.

Many of the rules are legal requirements and your disobedience will be punished by the withering gaze of the law. You may be fined, committed to a penal institution and forced into attendance of wickerwork workshops and/or Open University learning programmes if you disobey the omnipotent hand at the end of the long arm of the highway law.

Rules for pavements

General guidance

1. Usually situated next to roads and in most cases running parallel to them, **PAVEMENTS** are slightly raised surfaces (marked by a raised kerb) utilized by poor people who can't afford a car and have been relegated to travelling on foot. When mounting a **PAVEMENT** you should be aware of the following hazards:

- **Pedestrians are unable to accelerate quickly** and can be unwilling to move at the same speed as your car. You should regard them with the same attitude as bollards and cattle – not a terrific problem if you hit them, but be aware of issues with scratched paintwork and dents.
- **Street furniture** such as lamp-posts, telephone boxes, benches, pensioners and other obstructions: Zimmer frames and other mobility devices can sometimes get caught in the steering system and cause issues with vehicle control. If you notice a loss of control, a metallic scraping noise and a stream of sparks while driving at high speed on a **PAVEMENT**, you should pull over into the next available shop front and remove any unwanted wheelchairs and walking aids out from under the car.

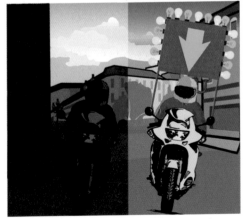

Be safe, be seen, unless you don't want to be seen, say if you've just done over a bank or something, in which case see p.34, paragraph 53 – Police Stopping Procedure

3

Rules for pedestrians

General rules

In addition to regulations and advice contained in the following section, further rules applying to pedestrians will be found throughout *The Myway Code*. Simply cross out the word 'car', 'lorry' or 'horse' and replace it with 'person' until you are struck by the sheer banality of the exercise in particular, or modern life in general.

| Black cab | Traffic police | Bastard |

Examples of vehicles

The underclass

| Roadkill | Stray dog | Higher simian | Pedestrian |

Your place in the scheme of things

Transport by means of ambulatory locomotion is something most of us are reluctantly drawn into at some point or another, so it's vital to remember just where walking places you in the road users' hierarchy. As you will see from the diagram above, it is quite near the bottom. In fact, there are only higher simians, stray dogs and the still-quivering limbs and fading consciousness of partially pressed roadkill to feel superior to in any respect.

2. Always use the pavement, where provided. Pavements and footways are secure areas provided to **SEGREGATE PEDESTRIANS** from vehicles weighing up to 20 tonnes by means of a 4-inch-high wall known as a kerb.

3. Pavements and footways are easily identifiable, even to the occasional pedestrian, and may be freely accessed provided you remember the following points:

- **You may join** the flow of pedestrian traffic at any point on the pavement – there is no need to give way or signal to other pavement users that you wish to join the footway. However, your journey will be safer if you do **EMPLOY A FLASHING LIGHT OR HAND SIGNAL** of some kind while performing pavement manoeuvres, as other pedestrians will maintain a safe distance from you – usually the approximate length of an outstretched arm clutching a bread knife.

- **Make sure you take enough rests.** Losing concentration through tiredness whilst out walking can lead to loss of control of your legs which can lead, in turn, to you crashing into shop windows or veering across the pavement into the path of an invalid carriage – possibly further maiming a cripple, which would be hard for you to deal with in terms of your latent guilt complex. Fortunately, like roads, many pavements are equipped with rest areas, known as **BENCHES**. Often provided in memory of the dead, these are consequently reserved for use by the nearly dead and may feature a little engraved plastic plaque that reads, e.g. *'For Gertie – who loved Rickmansworth High Street more than life itself'.*

- **Because there are no lanes,** separate carriageways or minimum speed requirements on the pavement, other pedestrians may behave in unpredictable ways, weave haphazardly from side to side or attempt to run you off the path. Some will simply stop without warning to chat to a friend, answer their mobile phone or **VACANTLY GAWP** at something in a shop window.

- **In wet weather,** watch out for oncoming pedestrians who are apparently water-soluble or have some kind of non-trivial allergy to rain because, even in a light city drizzle, they insist on using an umbrella that blocks their forward vision and can take your eye out like a **MARSHMALLOW IMPALED** on a kebab stick.

- **Pavement and footway law stipulates** that you **MUST NOT** step on the cracks.

4. If there is no pavement, you are advised to walk on the **WRONG** side of the road, which is the **RIGHT** side of the road, when facing the wrong way and traffic is on your left. If you **MUST** walk backwards, reverse the polarity of the last sentence and wear something bright so that paramedics can easily find you in the ditch you are bound to end up in. When dawdling along on the wrong/right side of the road you should take super-special extra care and:

- **Walk in single file,** thereby forming an orderly queue for death.
- **Keep close to the edge of the carriageway.** Britain's hedgerows are fascinating.

5. Be safe, be seen. At night, help other road users to see you by always wearing something reflective. If you do not possess any neon dayglo clothing try wearing a bathroom mirror around your neck, fix candles to your shoulders or wear £5's worth of **ARGOS BLING** and walk in a gangsta-stylee *(see over)* to draw the attention of the local constabulary, who will arrive in a blaze of light and small-arms fire and be pleased to escort you to the nearest police station. If, however, you find yourself caught out in the dark with nothing more reflective than a copy of Keats's *Ode to a Nightingale,* **YOU MUST** drop your trousers and moon passing cars to alert them to your presence.

How to walk

6. Walking is a required skill for all pedestrians, but you **MUST** take care to walk in a *Myway Code* **APPROVED FASHION,** or it will all end in tears, you mark our words. The following pedestrian modes, however, are **NOT AUTHORIZED** for use on Britain's pavements:

- **Dawdling.** A method of ambulatory shuffling popular with gawping tourists, students, pensioners, credulous buffoons and all other pedestrians without a clear itinerary. Like particles of saturated fat that clog up blood vessels, dawdlers cling to the side of the arterial flow, attaching themselves to shop windows and the entrances to tourist attractions. Gradually, other dawdlers join them, anxious to see what all the fuss is about, and before you know it the pavement is blocked like the coronary artery of a smoker superglued to a sofa made of fudge and force-fed lard in a hamburger restaurant.

- **Hassle-hustling.** The recommended mode of walking for busy business busybodies on business. Hassle-hustlers are on four-minute power-lunch breaks and are always, without exception, behind you, projecting their morally repugnant auras forward on carrier waves of French toiletries skilfully extracted from the musk glands of impossibly rare bijou oxen. Urgently pointing their suits at your shoulders and sighing like thwarted children, they are sometimes spotted in small herds hassling their way along the pavement three or four abreast wielding briefcases and an air of insufferable smugness.

- **Gangsta-stylee.** A massively overplayed waddle punctuated by unnecessary shoulder, knee and elbow twitches rendered absurd by jeans with ankle-height crotches and a padded coat liberated from its original purpose as an immersion-heater insulation jacket. Popular in da urbanzone, walking gangsta-stylee takes up approximately three times as much space as ordinary walking.
- **The sidewalk do-si-do.** Performed by two pedestrians approaching one another on a collision course and trying to move out of each other's way. This little pavement dance has three distinct phases. Five, if you count the recriminations and nosebleeds.

7. According to *Myway Code* research, the pavement is only as safe as the most deranged person on it. However, what dangers there are can be avoided by perfecting the skills of defensive walking. Before venturing out onto Britain's streets you should familiarize yourself with the following human hazards and take steps to avoid them at all costs:

- **Skateboarders.** When not spraying their tags on walls or **DISRESPECTING THEIR ELDERS,** disaffected skateboarding youths like nothing better than hanging around in preposterously baggy casual trouserwear and alienating the old and unfit by filming themselves performing death-defying leaps in bus stations using bits of old pallet and wheelchair ramps.

- **Joggers** come out of the office at lunchtime and spend the next 45 minutes running around in a huge circle back to the office. They are, therefore, just **PEDESTRIANS WITH NOWHERE TO GO** and condemned, despite their slightly increased velocity, to spend more time getting there than anyone else. The health benefits that joggers enjoy by running right up to the moment when they suffer a minor heart attack are offset by hyperventilating enough traffic fumes to simulate a 40-a-day Rothmans habit. Seemingly determined to die one way or the other, joggers often travel in pairs so that if their healthy lifestyle doesn't kill them they can, at the very least, try to bore one another to death. The main danger of joggers is not their speed, which is barely more than walking pace, but the **ANCILLARY FLAILING MOVEMENT** of elbows and clenched fists they employ to make them feel as if they are starring in *Chariots of Fire*.

- **Chuggers.** Charity muggers stand around with clipboards on city pavements and attempt to establish eye contact with the weak, the vulnerable and the self-consciously guilt-stricken. They aim to arrest your attention and then stop you for long enough to shame you into a tenner a month direct debit donation – which may, for example, enable a troupe of unicyclists to **ENTERTAIN ORPHANED BEARS** in Cambodia. Once they have your attention, through the underhand tactic of smiling or talking to you, you will be deluged with requests for your signature within moments, on account of their gittish grasp of street psychology and a smile so enthusiastic that seeing it for longer than five minutes will ignite the urge to thump it, repeatedly. Until one little thing that they say reveals that they have the moral complexity of a door-to-door vacuum-cleaner salesperson, and you can safely go back to regarding them with deep suspicion and be on your way.

Pedestrian crossings

8. Zebra crossings are a tried and trusted method of injecting excitement into every road-user's day. They are governed by unwritten laws which regulate a collection of symbolic dance moves by pedestrians which are, in turn, answered by a series of vehicle manoeuvres, building up to a climax of uncontrolled swerves.

- **Pedestrians** using Zebra crossings understand they may not reach the other side of the road without an act of bravado or defiance and the benefit of your insurer's rock-solid collision damage waiver.

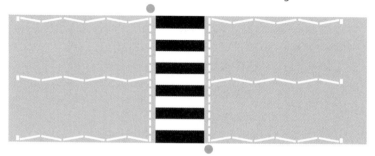

- **Beware** of so-called **EVIL TWIN ZEBRAS,** which are identical in every respect to a normal crossing, except that the black and white road markings are reversed. These counterfeit Zebras have no legal status whatsoever and are therefore just as dangerous as the real thing.

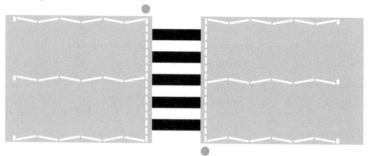

- **If you cross an Evil Twin Zebra** crossing, **YOU MUST** drive anti-clockwise around the nearest approved DSA test centre at high speed in reverse. Only this **WIDDERSHINS RITUAL** can counteract the Baneful and Nefarious Curse of the Great Zebrada.

- **Drivers should ensure that they are approaching the crossing** from the correct direction. If you attempt to use a Zebra crossing perpendicular to the normal flow, you may find pedestrians hurtling down the carriageway towards you at speeds of up to 30 mph.

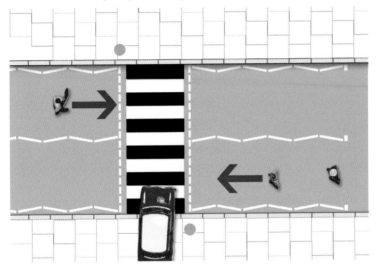

9. Pelican crossing

PELICAN stands for Pedestrian Electric Light Interface Craving an Abbreviated Name. A Pelican is a large pelagic bird capable, though usually unwilling, of carrying pedestrians in its beak pouch. Moreover it is closely related to the Zebra, though less dangerous, which is where the inspiration for the name comes from.

For the motorist, the sequence of lights at a Pelican crossing is broadly similar to that of a standard traffic light, the only difference being the flashing amber signal. A flashing amber light indicates that a driver is within his or her rights to aggressively rev the engine at the exact same frequency as the signal. The corresponding light for pedestrians at all new Pelican crossings has now changed from a flashing green man to a pulsating orange chicken.

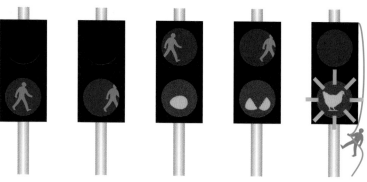

10. Toucan crossing

A new set of signals that allows cyclists, as well as pedestrians, to cross the proper traffic flow. So named because 'two can cross' at the same time, the Toucan also happens to be a large tropical bird with plumage markings that closely resemble two wide tyre tracks up its back.

CAPTAIN DEATH SAYS...

Remember

- **Be clean.** Make sure you are wearing fresh underwear before setting out on your journey.
- **Be safe** from so-called 'safety features'.
  Seatbelts trap you in burning cars.
  Airbags suffocate you when you're unconscious.
  Pedestrian crossings are the first place a homicidal motorist will choose for easy pickings.

Pontiff crossing

Years of research at the government's Pedestrian Safety Research Laboratory concluded that conventional Zebra crossings were simply not taken seriously enough for the purposes of pedestrian and driver safety, and that the Belisha beacon was not striking enough for today's visually sophisticated road user. Looking for an arresting icon that demands respect across all boundaries, ecumenical and secular, the Laboratory created the Pontiff crossing – a new roadside beacon that beseeches motorists to take the utmost care on their approach. The new Pontiff crossing incorporates the following road safety features:

- **Striking design.** 3-metre stroboscopic Pope ensures that motorists will not miss the approach to a pedestrian crossing again.
- **Flashing head and halo.** For high visibility in all weather conditions, including tempest and Biblical flood.
- **Papal animatronics.** Once cars have passed over the crossing, figure crouches to kiss the tarmac.

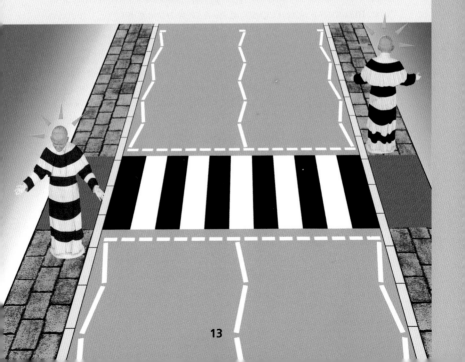

11. Puffin crossing

Similar to Pelicans and Toucans, except for the absence of a flashing amber signal, a Puffin crossing has special sensors that cancel the request to cross if the pedestrian has somehow dematerialized, taken their chance without waiting or has simply been taken out by a swerving high-sided vehicle.

12. Greenfinch crossing

An experimental pilot scheme where pedestrians follow a line of seeds and pine kernels across Britain's busiest roads.

Crossing roads

14. Where Zebra, Pontiff or light-controlled crossings do not exist you must rely on your own wits to get you across the road in one piece or, alternatively, you could always hire a car and drive to the opposite side of the road. In cases where car hire is impractical, pedestrians should familiarize themselves with the Other Side Code (see facing page). *(Rule 13 has been omitted for reasons of superstition.)*

15. Watch out for reversing vehicles. Remember that lorries go backwards as well as forwards and that buses go backwards as well as not at all. In addition to the standard white reversing light, lorries, buses and other commercial vehicles reversing may sound the following warnings:

- **A repetitive signal,** similar to the engaged tone you will hear if you ring up the *How Is My Driving?* helpline number, clearly visible under the vehicle's rear axle.
- **A spoken robotic voice,** usually repeating a key phrase along the lines of 'Stand back, vehicle reversing, assimilate, assimilate, you will all be assimilated.'
- **A crunching sound** not unlike the tyre of a heavy goods vehicle rolling over your torso.
- **An electronic medley of tones and bleeps** intimating that you will shortly be knocked down by a runaway amusement arcade.

Cross to the Other Side
with Captain Death

1 **Stop** and cross anywhere you like. You won't be able to see much from the pavement, so get out into the road to see past parked cars, large trucks, buses and roadworks.

2 **Using your skill and judgement,** as well as your need for extreme danger, walk in a weaving, diagonal line across the road, stopping to listen for traffic the old Comanche Way – by crouching down and pressing one ear to the ground.

3 **Do not bother to look.** As a pedestrian, your judgement of speed and distance is flawed and it is utterly pointless. Better to rely on your animal instincts.

4 **Remember** to defiantly sniff the air like an aroused badger. This will increase the mystique surrounding you and your forthcoming arrival on the Other Side.

5 **Listen out** for the swish of the scythe and 'Don't fear the Reaper'. Captain Death cares about your extinction experience.

CAPTAIN DEATH SAYS...

Other Side Code

Worried about crossing a busy road?

Well, worry no more, with the Other Side Code.

Captain Death is your magical guide,

And he's sure to assist you,

To the Other Side.

Rules for animals

General statement

No animals were harmed during the making of this section, though we did eat a bacon sandwich and may have trodden on some spiders.

The Myway Code defines an animal as a non-human biological entity that is not a plant, a member of the kingdom of fungi or a former heart-throb from a boy band, though in the case of the latter the rules for chains, leashes and cleaning up droppings are similar.

For the purposes of *The Myway Code,* animals fall into two groups:
- **Those** you believe you have control of, and
- **There are no others.** No animal is fully in your control. That little chihuahua may look like a crazy kind of dog that more or less does as it's told, but its inner voice tells it that it is a fully grown timber wolf, ready to bite the larynx out of your throat as soon as the Cesar dog food dish falls empty for a sufficient length of time. The fact that it licks your face just confirms this: it wants to eat you, it's just getting the taste for it.

16. Safety first. You can't trust a horse. Though beloved of pre-teenage girls, horses and ponies are unbelievably dense and irrational animals that, like the front page of the *Daily Mail,* oscillate wildly between the twin negative states of anger and fright. (Their third state, that of a strong and rather useful glue, occurs only after lengthy boiling.) A more positive view of horses is available in the journals of *Black Beauty* – quite smart for a horse, but still an atrocious writer.

The Myway Code states that you should avoid equine contact altogether except in the context of a healthy wager of several hundred pounds every year on the Grand National. The bet will at least reinforce your aversion to the deceitful, untrustworthy buggers and you will give them the wide berth they seem to need. Of course all of this is a moot point if you actually resemble a horse and Daddy doesn't mind buying hay for your only friend.

17. Riding a horse. If you must go horse riding, you should wear protective clothing at all times. There are a number of styles of protective clothing, depending on what kind of stupid horse riding you wish to participate in.

1 **Old money fox hunters.** Red coat, jodhpurs, riding hat and supercilious sneer perfect for the cold-blooded lobotomized toff out for an afternoon of issuing a damn good thrashing to the plebs.

2 **The Knight and the Princess.** This is the Disney-eye view of horses – specifically, horses from the cartoon age of chivalry, where men were men and women were basically so pathetic they were unable to do anything more complex than grow 20 feet of blonde hair and ride sidesaddle into a technicolor sunset on a Disney horse. Horses that, like medieval Princess Barbie, have no anus, are super-cuddly best friends and cannot hurt you because they are kind and love you in a non-alarming way. Not horses that could break both your legs, shit

on your face, eat all your sugar and then present you with Rolf
Harris's vet bill. No, not those horses at all, oh no.

18. Horses on the road. Driving where there are horse riders on the
road can be hazardous, particularly when you consider that the riders
are rarely in ultimate control of their animal. Fortunately, horses
themselves give off subtle signals about their intentions. Learning to see
these signs can help you become a better driver.

Horse signals from the rear

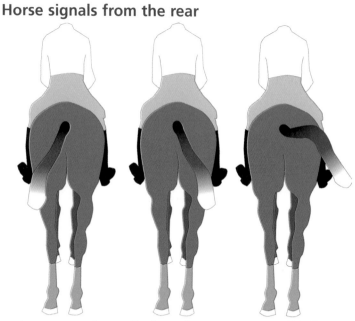

I may or may not
turn left or right at
next junction and/or
over the hedge.
Who can tell?

The fly crawling up
my back is about to
make me bolt off,
killing absolutely
everyone concerned.

I am on a high-fibre diet
and I will shortly be
taking a long and
satisfying dump
on your car bonnet.

19. Horse riders MUST NOT use footpaths – even when not riding –
as their bow-legged waddle can obstruct other pedestrians.

Dogs

20. While walking your dog, you should always pretend to be in full control even if, as is usually the case, you are not. For example, if your hound runs off the leash and attacks an orphan in the park you must always take the following action:

- **Shout** 'No Jaunty, stop being naughty' repeatedly until all the witnesses are out of earshot.
- **Tell the victim** that 'He's just being friendly but he must really, really like you' as you wrestle an ear lobe from the jaws of your dog.

21. Your dog must not bark on a road in a built-up area between the hours of 11 pm and 7.30 am unless it is alerting you to:

- **Someone** who has fallen down a well.
- **The impending escape** of a villain in a black cowboy hat from a corral or desert-based compound.
- **An imminent danger** that threatens the wellbeing of Champion the Wonderhorse.

22. Taking your dog in the car. Occasionally, dog owners like to ferry their diseased pets around, so that they can empty their bowels in different scenic locations. When carrying a dog by car:

- You **MUST NOT** let it reprogram the GPS head unit so that every journey somehow terminates at the Winalot factory.
- If you have a small dog, you **MUST NOT** let it run around inside the car in case it gets caught under the pedals.
- You **MUST NOT** let it perform any tricks based on a burning hoop.

23. Rule 23 has been withdrawn in order to promote a sense of mystery and intrigue among the numerologically literate, conspiracy theorists and other outright fools and nutters.

Instead, *The Myway Code* draws your attention to the route of the A23 and M23 around Gatwick Airport and invites you to draw your own conclusions about it all.

Cattle

Under the new rules of the latest *Myway Code* and food safety regulations, a herd of cows may only be allowed onto the road once each individual animal is fitted with a short leash held by a responsible adult in protective clothing. Each cow must also carry a label detailing the nutritional composition of the animal and a panel that clearly states **WARNING: MAY CONTAIN COW.**

24. Herding at night. You should normally herd cattle only by day, but where herding at night or in poor visibility is unavoidable, all animals **MUST BE** dressed in waterproof, high-visibility clothing, similar to that used by motorway maintenance crews. A hazard warning light is also advisable.

High-visibility cow coats are available from farm supply shops as well as many back-street party and fetish-wear manufacturers.

Sheep

Sheep are medium-sized animals of a haphazard disposition that display a degree of consciousness and intelligence akin to a bucket of suds. Like all other animals, therefore, they **MUST NOT** be trusted, let alone approached.

25. If you see sheep while driving, first check to make sure that you are not counting them as they jump over a fence one by one, that your eyes are not closed and that you do not have a warm cup of malted barley drink in your hands. **CAUTION:** The higher the number of sheep counted, the greater the degree of danger that awaits you upon opening your eyes.

25. (Cymru).
Dafad ydy achos buchedd mo jyst achos Nadolig.

Did you know?

- **Your dog** can only see in black and white, so cannot tell the difference between motorway and primary route signage.
- **Cats** have never been licensed. Because, unlike dogs, they've never had to worry about affording the more expensive option, they have always had the ability to see in colour as well as black and white.
- **Horses** are really, really stupid.

Rules for cyclists

General

In addition to those in the following section, certain extra rules apply to cyclists which you will find throughout *The Myway Code*. Look for the cyclon (cycle icon) in the margin or, alternatively, pretend you know everything, you smug, self-satisfied git.

26. Protection. Because you have little physical protection, you should cultivate an air of **PIETY AND RIGHTEOUSNESS** at all times. Together with your irrefutable ecological qualifications and militant smugness you will be able to generate a considerable Übermenschian forcefield around you powered purely by **MORAL SUPERIORITY.** Only then will you be able to confront the inevitable consequence of cycling, which is to be verbally abused, cut-up and generally run off the road.

27. Helmet. In the event of a fatal accident, a cycle helmet is an essential accessory that will protect your devout countenance in death, while making your head look like a mushroom at all other times.

28. Clothing. Despite being an alfalfa-chewing wholegrain eco-warrior, you should fight the urge to wear **HIPPY** clothing when riding a bicycle. Tassels and flimsy-filmy tie-dyed blouses can easily get caught in your chain as well as being deeply unfashionable. Your brightly coloured look-at-me haircut is useful for visibility, however. Despite marking you out in normal life as a circus freak tosser of the highest order, drivers will instinctively give you a wide berth as sure as if they were accidentally attending the same social function as you.

29. Cycling at night requires extra care. Your bicycle must be fitted with front and rear lights which may be powered by mains electricity or a battery. Cyclists who wish to employ a **DYNAMO** arrangement should first try cycling around in the dark with their brakes on to see if such an arrangement suits them.

In well-lit metropolitan areas, where post-twilight ambient light levels exceed **37.5 CANDLE POWER,** it is no longer necessary to carry lanterns to illuminate the road, though it is mandatory to use lighting to draw attention to yourself. Examples of suitable bicycle lighting in such areas therefore include front- and rear-mounted:

- Lava-lamps.
- Widescreen
  televisions receiving
  broadcasts of a gauche and/or
  garish nature, such as the
  entire BBC1 peak-time
  schedule (dimly lit dystopian
  drama is not allowed).
- Disco rope lights.
- Laser beams.

Examples of lighting that draws attention to the cyclist but is **NOT SUITABLE** include:

Using lava-lamps has the added advantage that you're no longer the only thing on your bike that looks like a dick.

- An arc-lamp swooping across the sky indicating the imminent threat of approaching enemy aircraft.
- Front- and rear-mounted police interrogations involving the use of an Anglepoise lamp.
- All other types of silliness.

30. Use cycle routes where possible. Cycle routes are built in such a way as to never be the shortest distance between two points. They pass through notoriously **VIOLENT HOUSING ESTATES** and toxic former industrial wastelands cheap enough to buy for the benefit of cyclists. As a cursory glance at your local council's cycle route map will surely convince you, **DRIVING WILL ALWAYS BE QUICKER** and will save you the bother and embarrassment of sacrificing your cycle to a knife-wielding group of eight-year-olds.

31. Cycle lane on conventional road. A narrow corridor along the nearside lane of a major primary route riddled with potholes, **DEAD MAGPIES,** dogshit and blocked drains which affords cyclists the opportunity to use real roads for a change. Cycle lanes are often surface-treated with peppermint tarmac to neutralize the stale odour of exercise and panic-induced sweat. In some cases, particularly where cyclists are required to share a lane with buses and taxis, the lane surface may be treated with red tarmac in order to disguise the blood.

32. When using cycle lanes:

- **Travel in a family group** of three or four with Dad at the front and the youngest child at the rear. This will remind other road users of mallards taking their ducklings to the relative safety of water for the first time, only you will be taking your children to Britain's most dangerous roundabout instead.
- **You may be provided with an advanced stop line** at traffic lights. This is a wide area of pink or peppermint tarmac where you will just be able to make out a white bicycle symbol under the tyres of a fat-arse four-wheel-drive bourge-mobile with bullet-proof glass and a driver who will kindly provide you with a definition for the word 'thumpable'.

Cycling was much safer when the roads were quieter. Back in the 1940s you could cycle around for miles and get home safely, just in time for diphtheria.

33. Traffic signs and signals are to be obeyed by all road users, including cyclists. This includes traffic lights, you facetious little box of turds. In particular cyclists must always:

- **Obey all instructions** except any that, in your pumped-up and antagonistic state of mind, you feel do not take account of your earnestly held opinions on what is wrong with Britain's roads. For instance, while technically illegal, cycling the wrong way up a one-way street, through a red light and over a disabled pedestrian may be considered an act of self-expression by the European Court of Human Rights. But only if you kill someone. Otherwise, apparently, it's just not art.

34. While cycling you should always:

- Hold the handlebars with both hands, except when eating a bag of crisps, gesturing to other road users or adjusting your gonads into their proper storage position at the base of the neck.
- Wear Lycra and behave like a fascist.
- Stop at traffic signals and pick fights with other road users.

- Expose your majestic, muscular, pulsating thighs for the personal enjoyment of other road users. You kinky devil.

35. While cycling you must never:
- Carry passengers unless they contribute to the effort of cycling. Any other way, madness lies.
- Take part in a jousting contest on the public highway.
- Cycle on a pavement and knock down old people unless you are swerving to avoid a more worthwhile member of society.

36. In addition, while cycling at speed you **MUST NEVER:**
- Get off.
- Attempt to catch flying birds with a butterfly net.
- Drop down a gear, or your legs will need to rotate at higher speeds, potentially sucking in parts of the hedgerow and smaller pedestrians.

37. After cycling for any length of time you **MUST:**
- Never attempt to walk in a place where deportment or gracefulness is essential as you will have developed the exotic waddle of John Wayne repeatedly tripping over a spacehopper.
- Seek out friends and colleagues who have some kind of olfactory deficiency, or those that simply enjoy the smell of other people's sweat.

38. Rule 38 has been withheld for reasons of space. If you find yourself being prosecuted under **Rule 38** and wish to appeal against the **MANDATORY DEATH PENALTY,** you may use one of the special coupons at the back of the book that entitle you to appeal for a stay of execution. Please see the Standards of Driving Office leaflet *The Death Sentence: How it Affects You* for more information.

Specialist cycle lanes
The Myway Code now allows road markings, including cycle lanes, to be changed from time to time. These changes are intended to reflect no-

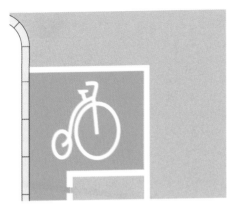

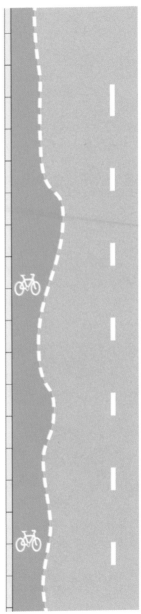

frills, real-world conditions, as agreed during meetings convened in our walnut- and leather-lined penthouse offices, where ministers, staff and their houseboys are ferried in via helicopter. Two of the changes are outlined below:

- **Penny-farthing lanes** *(above)* will be phased out by 2028.
- **Wobbly lanes** *(right)* will be phased in for certain sections, based on the random path deviation of cyclists accelerating uphill, or away from lights.

Road junctions

Negotiating road junctions is a particular hazard for cyclists as it represents a very real chance for other road users to get the better of them. You may prefer to dismount and wheel your bicycle across the junction, but will be laughed at by everyone, including the lowest-of-the-low – the pedestrians whose ranks you have now joined, you hopeless self-loathing loser.

Rules for motorcyclists

General

The following section contains rules and regulations for motorcyclists in charge of a vehicle that exceeds the power output of a hand-held hairdryer. It does not include scooters. Scooterists should read the section on cycling while manoeuvring a 1950s upright vacuum cleaner for a flavour of the law as applied to their vehicles.

39. Do not perform tricks on the public road system unless they serve a higher purpose. Your one-inch wheelies may impress the bored, teenage occupants of a village bus shelter, but things have moved on somewhat and, in order to die a heroically reckless and futile death, you now need to hurtle towards your demise in a more socially responsible manner. Examples of acceptable stunts include:

- **Decongestion charge.** You ride full throttle in the 'environmental saviour' position *(below left)* into oncoming traffic which swerves out of your way, thereby alleviating congestion.

- **Motorway flyover.** Entertain queueing drivers on the M25 by leaping lines of stationary cars *(above right)*.

40. You must not carry any passenger on a motorcycle unless it is an inappropriately tattooed woman in a bikini.

41. Daylight riding is against the law of the **DARK LORD SAURON.** Your motorcycle is only rideable during daylight hours on the A666 where marked with the Sign of the Beast *(see right)*.

42. Riding in the dark. Stick Slayer on your iPod and forget about wearing anything reflective. It will only minimize your ability to induce terror in other road users, which, let's face it, is the whole point of riding a motorcycle.

43. Manoeuvring. A motorcycle not moving at speed is as graceless as a tap-dancing elephant seal. Do not attempt to turn in a confined space unless no one is looking, otherwise you may damage your image – that you are a **RAGING WARRIOR RIDING A STEED OF THE DAMNED.**

The Dark Lord commandeth: STAY IN LANE

Motorways

Motorcycle enjoyment is directly proportionate to the likelihood of death while riding. So motorways are the only roads worth riding on.

There are certain items of clothing you can purchase to give yourself enough of an impression of safety to actually be prepared to ride a motorcycle on a motorway, but in reality they offer no protection at all. Imagine if you were about to be attacked by a maniac wielding an industrial sander. Would you really defend yourself by wrapping your body in clingfilm and putting a bucket on your head?

The only truly safe way to ride a motorcycle is to ride one around the front room of a house a teenager is holding a party in (without the permission of their parents). Then you will appear frightening and brave without actually having to risk your life.

Rules for drivers and motorcyclists

44. Before setting off make sure that:
- Your vehicle has wheels. Attempting to move in a vehicle without wheels could prove to be frustrating.
- You have some idea of where you are going.
- You are not wearing a hospital robe and/or are bleeding.
- You are facing the way you intend to travel.
- You have fuel, crisps and fizzy pop.

45. Vehicle towing

You **MUST NOT** drive a tow truck unless you have appeared in a tabloid magazine under the headline 'I was a trucking **BIGAMIST**' for having three wives based in different parts of the country. Extra loadage can be applied for if, despite your public humiliation, you successfully kept from the journalist details of your families in Poland and Azerbaijan.

You **MUST NOT** use an old pair of trousers to tow a caravan instead of the appropriate tow bar. You could do in the old days but they just don't make trousers like they used to.

Seatbelts

46. You must wear a seatbelt unless you want people to say 'What a complete twat. If only he'd worn a seatbelt he wouldn't be dead' at your funeral.

Fitness to drive

47. It may hinder your driving ability if you have recently broken both arms, just had corrective eye surgery or are in the process of having sexual intercourse. (It is your duty to inform the VDLA if you have caught a sexually transmitted disease while driving so that they can all laugh about it during their lunch hour and wink at each other when you come in to revalidate your licence.)

Alcohol and drugs

48. Anyone considering driving while under the influence of drink or drugs should read the following testimonials from a random selection of young club-goers:

'I knew I shouldn't have driven when I came up to a junction and couldn't remember how to get home. In the end I decided to take the road on the left rather than the rainbow one going up into the sky.' – **Geoffrey**

'I racked my brain about what *The Myway Code* said drivers should do in the event of pink hippos abseiling down the inside of your windscreen and running off to gambol in the rainforest.'

– **George**

'Sshvdriiive? You fuskin, shupin crazeeeee? Fuccch off zchu kaaant!'
– **Bungle**

Remember

- **Drugs don't mix with driving.** Your vehicle is not fitted with a proton drive and you must not park on the moon.
- **Warp power is not fitted** as standard on the hatchback. That mysterious slider with the fan-like symbol on it is the fan.
- **Drinking and driving** marks you out as an unreconstructed, prehistoric git of the lowest order.

Rules for drivers

Read this chapter carefully. Knowing the rules of the road will give you the confidence to patronize other road users at all times.

If the car in front of you is not going as fast as it possibly can you should attempt to run it off the road. Hesitation from other drivers should be interpreted as weakness and be exploited whenever it occurs. If enough drivers took seriously the duty of scaring spineless drivers then all people of a timid disposition would get out of their cars and back on public transport where they belong (newly qualified drivers or NQDs are a particular nuisance). This will leave the roads clear for **REAL DRIVERS** and in turn reduce the amount of accidents on Britain's roads. It sounds fascistic but it's really just about safety.

The three most important words in the driver's handbook are therefore **INTIMIDATION, INTIMIDATION** and **INTIMIDATION**. It is the solemn duty of all drivers to cultivate high levels of terror in all other road users for the reasons set out above.

Signals

49. Signals sometimes communicate your actions to other road users. There is no need to signal if there are no other cars around you. Pedestrians and cyclists don't count. **IT'S YOUR ROAD, NOT THEIRS.**

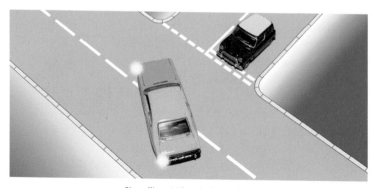

Signalling: What is the point?

Signals are only really used by new drivers anyway. As you become more experienced at driving you will realize that signalling only confuses people. If you are driving fast enough, everyone will be clear about where you're going and what you intend to do. The best signal to give other drivers is that you are a hard, slightly psychotic bastard and it would be best for them if they just got out of your way.

Don't forget that shouting and hammering your horn are signals too. Indeed, 'Get out of the bloody way' is a phrase that can be used in almost every circumstance, rendering indicators useless.

Arm signals may also be appropriate, see the relevant *Myway Code* leaflet *Offensive Hand Gestures When Driving Abroad* for more details.

50. You may find that cars around you insist on relying on signals to notify you of their intentions, but you also have to assume they will not do what their signal suggests. Just be confident and plough on regardless of what their 'signals' may seem to imply. The only signal you need to worry about is the one other drivers get from your exhaust pipe as you leave them choking in your dust.

51. Policemen and traffic wardens may signal to you when you are driving. Policemen have the power to put you in **PRISON** and take away your driving licence, thus forcing you into the ignominy of public transport. So it's best to pay attention to them. It has also been said that people forget traffic wardens are human beings, and that we should treat them with courtesy and respect. This is wishy-washy **LIBERAL BOLLOCKS**. Traffic wardens get bonuses for fining people merely for stopping at a bus stop for half an hour while they do their shopping. I mean what kind of country are we living in if a sodding bus passenger gets priority over people who own cars? Doesn't anyone know anything about status any more? Just for the record, people with cars are better than people who get the bus, and for God's sake, being an unemployed benefit cheat is better than being a traffic warden.

52a. Traffic lights for drivers

Drivers have brains, otherwise they wouldn't have passed their driving test, so there is no need to patronize them by explaining the traffic light sequence. If only the same could be said for **SODDING** cycle couriers.

52b. Traffic lights FOR SODDING CYCLE COURIERS

Let's take this slowly shall we? After all anyone can ride a bike on the road, the so-called cycling *proficiency* test is a joke. A red light on a set of traffic lights means 'STOP'. Apply your brakes and do not pedal or move at all. Your bike should be stationary for the duration of the light being red. A red light on a set of traffic lights does not mean STOP for people in cars (who, while we're on the subject, actually pay for the bloody roads that you get to use for free) but GO for people on bikes. Neither does a red light on a set of traffic lights mean, 'Edge out if nothing is coming and go even though it's not your turn to move.' In fact, let's break this down even further. Traffic lights actually **MEAN** something. They are not just there because they look pretty. If you'd rather not end up mangled under a cab then stop when the lights are red and only go when the lights are green. Jesus wept. And what's with all those piercings and tattoos? You look **STUPID**.

53. Police stopping procedure

If the police want to stop your vehicle they will. If you don't want to end up like Butch Cassidy and the Sundance Kid (dead) then do whatever they tell you to do.

54. Flashing your headlights

Do not flash your headlights unless you:
- **Fancy the person** driving in front of you.
- **Want to ask the person** driving in front of you if they'd like a fight.

55. If another driver flashes you with their headlights and you don't want to have sex with them or a fight, ignore them completely. If you would like to have sex with them or it is quite a long time since you had a scrap then pull over at the next available opportunity. Once you have pulled over you have only a few seconds to check whether you have misread the other driver's intentions.

56. Driving with the HORN
Driving with the horn can notify other road users of your presence, but only if you are particularly well endowed. It is best not to drive with the horn. Staring at pedestrian eye candy when you should be concentrating on the road can also be dangerous.

57. Lighting
At night you must always drive with your headlights on, unless you want to scare the shit out of one of your mates by creeping up behind them.

You **MUST NOT** suddenly switch on fog lights because it may dazzle other road users, unless you want to freak out one of your mates, in which case may we suggest driving up behind them without any lights on and then suddenly switching on your fog lights. This is one of the classic comedy driving moves.

Always dip headlights and traction beams on lonely country roads.

58. Hazard warning lights
It is a good idea to turn these on:
- **Whenever you park illegally.**
- **If you have broken down,** though most proper drivers would prefer not to draw attention to such humiliation.
- *The Myway Code* recommends that you should drive around with hazard lights on permanently if you have just passed your test.

Control of the vehicle

59. Braking in normal circumstances

If you need to be told how to brake, then you should only be allowed on the road if you're inside a bus.

60. Braking in an emergency

Oh for God's sake, we'll be telling people how to wipe their arses next.

61. Skids

WHAT? Oh ... not that kind of skid. Skidding looks cool and sounds cool too. It was pretty impressive on a bike but just imagine how awesome it feels in a car! Skidding is, however, quite tricky. It is best practised in a supermarket car park at night in someone else's vehicle. If you find yourself skidding **DO NOT** turn into the skid because that will stop you skidding and it will look as if you didn't do it on purpose.

In order to simulate the visual effect of a skid, *The Myway Code* illustrator was installed in a car with a box of pens. The car was then pulled sideways at high speed until the illustrator agreed not to have any more stupid illustration ideas.

62. Coasting

This word isn't in the dictionary, which goes to prove that dictionaries know nothing about cars. Make of that what you will. Coasting means you haven't got your car in gear. It means you are not in control of your car. Coasting means you've just passed your test and you will probably **CRASH** within the next seven days.

Lines and lane markings

63. Broken white lines

These are often found in the middle of the
road because that's what they are for, to
show where the middle of the road is. They
also act as perforations when the road needs
to be dug up and repaired.

64. Two white lines with the one nearest you broken

This means the road you are travelling on is
part of a huge morse code message that can
only be read from space.

65. Two white lines where the line on your side is solid

This means the council needed to use up their
spare supplies of white paint. It also means
drivers coming the other way may require you
to veer into a ditch so they can ovetake a
vehicle dawdling along their side of the road.

66. Diagonal white stripes (chevrons)

These slightly raised arrows are designed to
damage the suspension of vehicles that drive
over them. You can tell if you are driving on
chevrons because your car will judder slightly
and you will soon have to veer wildly to
prevent yourself ploughing into the **CENTRAL
RESERVATION**.

67. Lane dividers

Drive between the lines and you won't hit
other cars.

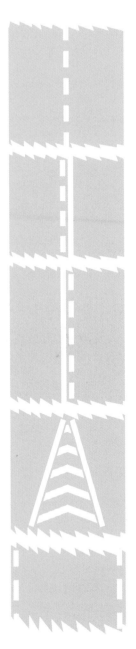

68. Reflective road studs

This is not an area for attractive men to congregate while examining the direction their lives have taken. Reflective road studs are there because they look pretty on a background of otherwise nondescript grey tarmac. They are like little jewels sparkling in the night sky that guide travellers on the highway of life.

Multi-lane carriageways

69. Lane discipline. It is a well-known fact that if everyone drove at 130 miles per hour there would be no accidents on the roads at all. If someone is deliberately sitting in the outside lane at 70 miles per hour then it is permissible to undertake on the inside. As you accelerate make angry gestures with your fists and project spittle on the inside of your window to convey your extreme agitation. To tell if you are doing this correctly look out for a stinging pain in your upper arm, a throbbing sensation in your forehead and then finally an aching sensation at the top of your chest.

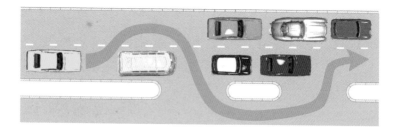

70. If you find yourself stuck in a traffic jam, weaving from one lane to another will alleviate boredom and keep other road users on their toes. The hard shoulder or even the other carriageway can be used if you are simply too busy to be kept waiting.

If you recently joined a motorway and find yourself stuck, simply reverse back up the hard shoulder, do a handbrake turn and drive confidently through the middle of any oncoming traffic, ignoring the screams.

71. Cycle lanes are usually painted on dual carriageways because the local council has targets for the cycle lane mileage it must provide within its boundaries. Cheaply sticking an extra white line on a dual carriageway neatly circumvents their need to actually provide useful routes where they are needed in towns. These cycle lanes should under no circumstances actually be used by anyone travelling on a bicycle. Cycle lanes that **SHOULD** be used are marked out by their accessibility. The ones on dual carriageways rarely have an entrance or exit point, thus underlining their complete and utter futility.

For this reason, cars may just use them to park in if drivers fancy stretching their legs.

72. Bus and tram lanes

Bus and tram lanes have monopolized important stretches of the road that car drivers used to be able to access. Unless you have one of the official car disguise kits available from *Myway Code* HQ ('Tram Suit' and 'Bus Suit') you will be fined for driving in these lanes.

Dual carriageways

73. Straddling both lanes gives you the opportunity to drive much faster than circumstances normally allow. If you see drivers sticking to the left or right lanes just

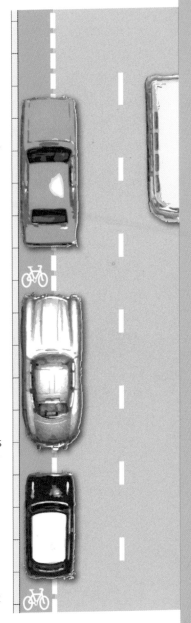

weave around them and go **'ERRRRRRR, ERRRR, ERRRRR'** increasing your vocal pitch as you go to emulate the sound of a Formula One car. Hopefully you will come across other drivers doing the same because this will give you the opportunity to have the 'duel' mentioned in the name of these roads.

74. Some dual carriageways have three lanes. Increase your speed accordingly.

75. One-way streets are a complete mystery. Informing you that you can only drive one way is absurd – you can only drive in one direction after all. This must have something to do with the parallel universes hypothesized in quantum physics.

General advice

76. You MUST NOT:

* Murder anyone.
* Covet your neighbour's wife.
* Expect to cook perfect poached eggs without using really fresh ones.
* Warm bottles of red wine by the fire, it won't warm it evenly. Try immersing it in warm water for three minutes instead.
* Attempt to clean the genital area with a brillo pad or twigs.
* Expect men to ask you about your day when you get home from work.
* Bore people with details about your loveless marriage.

General advice while driving

77. Satellite navigation systems, or **SAT NAV** as they are known by pubescent employees of Dixons, can be very helpful if you wish to plot re-entry to Earth following a mission to Mars to recover the Beagle probe in your Citroën C5. Otherwise they are strictly for taxi drivers only, who, owing to their unparalleled knowledge of Britain's entire road network, have developed the ability to drive without the need to ever actually look where they are going.

They may be all very well for finding your way through the Van Allen Belts, but satellite navigation systems cannot help you get to Nether Wallop.

78. Mobile phones

It is now illegal to hold anything in your hand other than the steering wheel while driving. This includes hand-held microphones, so forget those in-car karaoke sessions. You may talk on a mobile phone but only if you have one of the new 'hands free' steering wheels, which allow you to drive your car with your knees. Alternatively you may wish to buy a Bluetooth headset, but you should be aware of its drawbacks:

- You'll look like a wazzock.
- You may be unwittingly drawn into a *Star Trek* convention.
- You may find yourself singing backing vocals for Madonna.

79. In-car technology. In-car technology is a growth industry with a whole new generation of In-car-tainment prototypes soon coming on to the market. These include the **IN-CAR GYMNASIUM** – incorporating the in-car steam room facility; swimming cars, which give you the chance to practise your breast stroke while you're on the way to work; and perhaps most exciting of all, **GASTRO CARS,** which include a celebrity chef-endorsed kitchen installed on the back seat – allowing you to soufflé while you take the kids to school.

80. In slow-moving traffic.

Even though you are unable to move more than a few inches at a time it has to become second nature for you to move immediately into any space that becomes available in the road ahead. Rev your engine, release the clutch and lurch forward the second the car in front moves away.

If the driver in front does not fill the space in front of **HIS** car straight away then it is advisable to attempt an overtaking manoeuvre. Don't worry if there is not enough room for your vehicle to squeeze into – the etiquette of road use means he will have to give way to pay for his lack of attention.

Driving in towns
81. Towns are the peculiar congregations of different-coloured derelict structures that appear occasionally beside single-lane roads. In the olden days they contained things called 'communities' but now they consist

Stopping distances

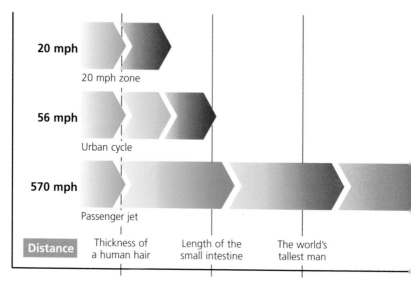

20 mph

20 mph zone

56 mph

Urban cycle

570 mph

Passenger jet

| Distance | Thickness of a human hair | Length of the small intestine | The world's tallest man |

largely of charity shops and estate agents. You may see ghostly shapes drifting aimlessly around these areas, listlessly throwing bricks through windows. These are young people who have nothing to do. You may ask why, if they have nothing to do, they insist on destroying the environment around them. It's because where they live is horrible and they consequently have no more respect for it than you do.

If you come across one of these 'towns' when out driving in your car, under no circumstances stop your vehicle. If you wish to take part in the act of spending money simply proceed to the next roundabout and follow signs for the nearest 'Superstore'. These 'Superstores' are new towns that are only accessible by car. They are shopping areas that have been sanitized and will not contain people who may offend you.

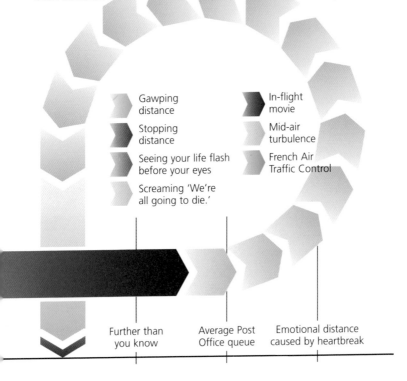

Gawping
distance

In-flight
movie

Stopping
distance

Mid-air
turbulence

Seeing your life flash
before your eyes

French Air
Traffic Control

Screaming 'We're
all going to die.'

Further than
you know

Average Post
Office queue

Emotional distance
caused by heartbreak

82. Traffic-calming measures

Prevalent in towns and villages inconsiderately located in the path of major roads, traffic-calming measures are designed to calm traffic by aggravating drivers. The first calming measure, the **SLEEPING POLICEMAN,** was so named to compensate for the rage these raised

humps induce in the driving public. By imagining you are running over a policeman, it is hoped that some of the anger and agitation you feel will be dispersed.

Recently, the science and art of traffic calming has reached new levels of both sophistication and irritation, seeking not only to calm but also to wilfully obstruct and confuse traffic. Modern in-town road surfaces feature many obstacles, including halt barriers, the carriageway tree, gun emplacements, sleeping nuns, the deep-textured surface de-elevation feature (a large hole in the road) and the new infinite roundabout, designed to divert all town centre traffic down a one-way no through road which terminates in a roundabout with no exits.

83. Town Centre Madness Zones (TCMZ).

These new schemes have been introduced by some urban councils to calm traffic relatively. By paying a small team of determinedly appalling motorists to veer around the road unpredictably, jump red lights and stop at random intervals, it is hoped to persuade other drivers to proceed with greater caution, thereby self-compensating for the utter madness. Council-appointed and licensed TCMZ drivers are also available for private hire, wherever you see the 'taxi' sign.

Obstruction and confusion measures

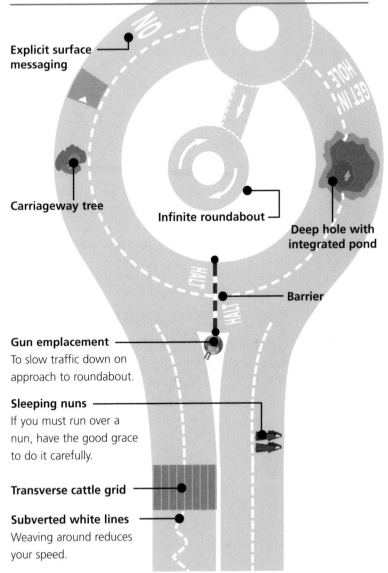

Explicit surface messaging

Carriageway tree

Infinite roundabout

Deep hole with integrated pond

Barrier

Gun emplacement
To slow traffic down on approach to roundabout.

Sleeping nuns
If you must run over a nun, have the good grace to do it carefully.

Transverse cattle grid

Subverted white lines
Weaving around reduces your speed.

General rules and advice for all motorists and other road users

Driving around

84. Before moving off into traffic you **MUST:**

- **Check that you want to go somewhere.**
  Government statistics show that it is actually safer to stay wherever you are than embroil yourself in the untidy and hazardous lives of the cretinous hoi polloi.
- Arrange all your mirrors so that light from outside your car travels through every known point in your personal universe, i.e. inside your car.
- Perform an inspection under the car to check for fluffy kittens playing gaily with a ball of wool, very short children or saboteur mechanics patiently cutting your brake lines.
- Switch on your hazard lights and bellow 'Is there anybody there?' from the offside window.
- Always remember the 13-point Ministry of Transport Acrostic Haiku.

Find your car
Access the driver's seat
Turn on the ignition
Accelerate wildly
Let out clutch pedal

Attempt wheelspin
Crash
Cry uncontrollably
Indicate
Drive into a nearby wall
Endeavour to remain conscious
No legs
Tough it out

Congratulations. You are now ready to commence your journey and take your chances in the world of buffoons and nincompoops that is the British driving public.

85. While you are driving and your vehicle is in motion you must:
- Always drive on the left side of the road, unless road markings, signals or those voices in your head specify otherwise.
- Remember other drivers are less competent than you.
- Be aware of other drivers and attempt to run them off the road.
- Take notice of cyclists and motorcyclists and feel inherently superior in every way.
- Dress comfortably and wear sensible shoes at all times, even when not driving.

86. Additionally, while driving you **MUST NEVER:**
- Open the offside door to ventilate the car following an over-rich rectal soliloquy resulting from last night's curry.
- Eat snacks or meals with high levels of participant involvement, such as fondues, tortilla wraps or in-car barbecues.
- Take up a diverting hobby.
- Construct or operate an 00 Gauge railway network or slot-car racing game on the back seat of your vehicle as this may lead to confusion.

- Operate a sewing machine, unless you are the rider of an Italian scooter and close inspection of the engine reveals you are actually driving a sewing machine.
- Shout 'What's the point of it all' and career across the road into the path of oncoming juggernauts.
- Stick your head out of the sunroof and spit at pedestrians.

Driving at night and in reduced visibility

You should be extra careful when driving in reduced visibility, at night or in reduced visibility at night.

87. At night, you **MUST NOT:**

- Switch your lights on before it is dark, or you won't feel the benefit.
- Wear pyjamas, use a feather pillow, snuggle up in a duvet or attempt to get into a sleeping bag. Police officers carry special equipment to determine the tog rating of the inside of your vehicle.
- Listen to the Radio 4 Shipping Forecast. In particular, listening beyond South Cromarty is extremely hazardous in a warm car and may result in loss of consciousness before Ronaldsway.
- Wear sunglasses. In particular, mirror shades will mark you out as an extraordinarily pretentious shitbag of the lowest order.

88. In reduced visibility, such as mist or fog, you should make sure that:

- You are not featuring in a romantic flashback sequence of a lightweight Hollywood romantic comedy.
- You are not wearing a stocking to obscure your features during an armed robbery attempt.
- You are not trying to drive a shower cubicle.
- You have not inadvertently driven onto the stage of a prog-rock reunion concert with its 8-inch cloud of dry ice. If you have, be sure to run over the lead guitarist as they are all, without exception, prancing gits.

89. If none of the above apply, you may drive at your normal death-defying speed and rely on everyone else to remain sensible. However, you should take care not to:

- Drive wearing glasses with frosted lenses or equivalent prescription designed to **CURE A TENDENCY TO PANIC** in the nervously fragile.
- Boil a kettle in the car.
- Beat yourself violently about the head with a heavy implement.

- Wear your spectacles back-to-front.

Controlling your vehicle

90. You must keep both hands on the steering wheel at all times except in the following cases of need:

- To salute members of the Royal Family or of Her Majesty's Privy Council that you may pass from time to time.
- To turn off a radio station that features a love song rendered by Mr Philip Collins in a way that may alter the balance of your mind sufficiently to contemplate an act of homicide.
- To attack said in-car entertainment device with a hammer if you have reasonable cause to fear a repeat incident and/or a serious Mariah Carey escalation.
- To stir your tea where sugar has been added but clockwise agitation has fallen short of agreed targets.
- To urgently complete the knitting of a jumper where failure to do so would otherwise result in a tank-top.

Road junctions

91. In the days of the Romans, roads just went in a straight line. It didn't occur to them to have junctions, which just goes to show that they weren't as clever as people say they were. Junctions are where two roads meet. Consequently they are dangerous. When approaching a junction you **MUST ALWAYS** remember:

- To look out for pedestrians. If they are crossing the junction you wish to turn into press your horn firmly and shout as loudly as you can. This will make them move across quickly enough to prevent you having to adjust your speed.
- Beware of cyclists. Lycra is something young people can get away with wearing if they have lumps in the right places. The same cannot

always be said of cyclists. Under the decency laws, children in your car may need to avert their gaze if a cyclist approaches.

- When exiting a junction, vehicles may indicate to show you the direction they wish to travel. They may also indicate because they have accidentally knocked their indication lever while reaching for a packet of m&m's in their glove box. They may even indicate because they don't know what their indicating lever is for, or just because it looks nice. Either way, drive according to other cars' indicators at your peril.

92. When exiting a junction advanced drivers should always wheel-spin just to prove that they can.

93. Some junctions have signs that say **STOP**. This means you should stop.

94. At road junctions, you should:
- Expect the unexpected. Many accidents are caused by a failure to master basic clairvoyancy skills.
- Always turn left unless the road junction is grade-separated and you have a police escort.
- Inform the gentleman who is walking ahead of you carrying a red flag of your intentions so that he may indicate these in an appropriate manner, thereby avoiding undue distress to the ladies and gentlefolk of your town.

95. Dual carriageways
Turning right across a dual carriageway is a bloody nightmare. There's a very strong chance that someone will career up your rear end and cause an enormous pile-up. God knows why we put turnings in such places. It's usually just for some hoity-toity's driveway, or else it's a road serving some random bit of countryside that no one ever goes down.

If you have to turn right because you are a hoity-toity and it's your driveway, or because you want to smoke marijuana with your friends but you all still live with your parents and need somewhere secluded, then for goodness sake just carry on to the next roundabout and turn round.

Box junctions

96. Thinking outside the box junction. Box junctions have yellow lines that criss-cross in a lovely pattern. The rules governing box junctions are purposely contradictory and vague in order to create maximum confusion in all NQDs and foreign drivers. In reality box junctions are governed more by philosophy than rules. Remember, **THEY ARE LIKE DOGS AND CAN SMELL FEAR.**

Like astrology, the way you approach a box junction will depend on a random sequence of interplanetary movements and personal aptitudes that accompanied the behaviour of your mother during your birth. There are a number of alternative methods of approach, based on ancient strategic games, while strategies based on oriental esoterica are emerging from the East. In any of the following cases, you should not attempt to choose an approach. The approach will choose you.

97. The chess approach. Primarily used when a black cab (Rook) seeks to turn right behind a white van (King) that is also turning right, but

Potential right turns from a Chess Box Junction after Bishop to Rook 4.

from the opposite direction. The opposing pieces negotiate the junction using an *obverse castling* move. There is a time limit – controlled by lights – and the *Dragon Variation* of the *Sicilian Defence* is allowed. *The Myway Code* states that all other vehicles turning right should be regarded as Knights, and pedestrians as hapless pawns.

98. The go approach. Becoming increasingly popular, this approach to box junctions stems from the ancient Chinese game of the same name – a board game broadly based on the principles and strategies of war. Many so-called road rage incidents have lately turned out to be little more than impromptu *go* tournaments fought out where multiple rights of way have not been sorted out since ancient times.

In order to win this junction, you must mobilize the orange cones to surround the yellow ones while retaining influence with the appropriate highway agency.

A classic *go* strategy would seek to remove rights of way from other drivers by the careful placement of traffic cones and diversion signs on the junction. In order to win, you must pull strings with the appropriate highway maintenance agency in advance of approaching the junction.

99. The holistic approach. Drawing on Eastern and Western oracular traditions, this approach requires the concentration of a Taoist monk *or* an advanced motoring instructor. After seven years of spiritual training, at the end of which they are able to drive a 4x4 over tissue paper without leaving a tear, these Tarmacadamite adepts literally 'become' the road and meditate themselves into the very fabric of the highway universe. The growing numbers of Tarmacadamites are evident in the oriental names of cars they choose to drive – the *Mitsubishi Shogun,* the *Ford Ka* and the *Range Rover Dalai Lama Edition.*

For Tarmacadamite monks, all box junctions appear as this wheel of life with integrated mini-yin-yang-roundabout. While only slightly more complex than a standard box junction, this layout accommodates seven different traffic flows and an infinite number of past lives.

100. Junctions controlled by traffic lights
These 'junctions' require no concentration and are therefore no fun at

all. Go if it is **GREEN** and do not go if it is **RED**. It's child's play.
If we carry on in this vein we'll all end up in electric cars while conveyor
belts herd us to and from work like so many mindless ants, reflecting
dolefully on the banality of life.

In days of yore there were no traffic lights and hardly any cars. It was
like the Wild West, with stand-offs at junctions where drivers acted with
mindless bravery and cunning to outwit their opponents and get ahead
of the pack. There were no rules, just the occasional danger of straying
into an episode of *Miss Marple*, which is where the upsurge in road
fatalities began. You may strike it lucky and come up to a junction that's
controlled by traffic lights only to find that the lights aren't working.
COUNT YOURSELF LUCKY if chance looks so kindly on you. Feel the
surge of adrenalin and draw upon your instincts to proceed. You have
seen but a glimpse of the Golden Age of road travel.

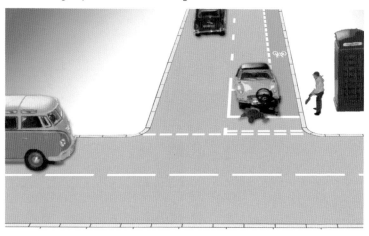

101. Advance stop lines. More and more junctions now have
advanced stop lines to allow bicycles to get in front of cars and buses at
traffic lights. This is due to the politically correct nature of modern life

and serves no beneficial practical application whatsoever. They actually make cyclists less safe. I mean, who's going to move off quicker, a car and a bus or a bicycle?

102. Roundabouts. When you approach a roundabout check to see if you have to slow down. It's much better if you don't, then you can achieve the extra momentum of performing a slingshot exit.

The slingshot exit

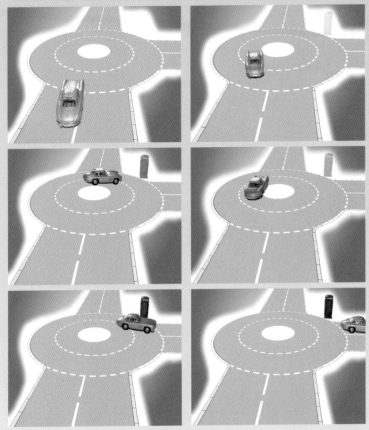

There may be many lane options at the approach to a roundabout. It doesn't really matter which one you take: the middle one is usually a safe bet for whichever turning you require. Then you've got all bases covered.

Signal if you want, but it might cause other drivers to assume you have recently passed your test and give them the uncontrollable urge to cut you up.

If a car is already on the roundabout then you should, strictly speaking, give it right of way. But if you feel it is travelling too slowly, or that you could just squeeze in front of it, go ahead. Cutting up nervous road users will increase your confidence, and we all know how important that is when driving.

You should go around a roundabout **CLOCKWISE** in the northern hemisphere and **ANTICLOCKWISE** in the southern hemisphere.

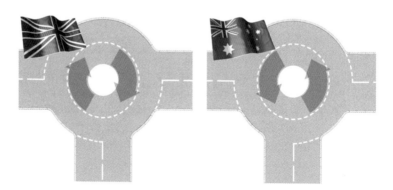

Once on the roundabout accelerate and turn the steering wheel towards the direction you wish to travel. If any car looks as though it may be about to drive across you, hammer your horn and veer into their path to scare them off.

103. You may see pedestrians on roundabouts. They will either be deranged or suicidal. Give them a wide berth. If you think cyclists and horse riders use the roads with an unfathomable air of peculiarity wait till you see one on a roundabout. They just go where they like, wobbling and swerving wherever the mood takes them. Some cyclists just use roundabouts as if they are driving a car. Curb your instincts and give these cyclists respect. They are hard.

104. Mini-roundabouts are absurd. Laugh heartily when you see drivers driving **AROUND** the painted white circle on the road as if it would damage their car if they drove across it. Continue laughing as you drive straight across it in front of them, cutting them up in the process.

Mini-roundabouts – just drive across the centre, you great jessy.

105. Multiple mini-roundabouts. Often given as incontrovertible proof that road designers have a sense of humour, multiple mini-roundabouts exist precisely because road designers **MUST NOT** have the faintest glimmer of a sense of humour if they are to do their job of skilfully thwarting the motorist at all times.

Overtaking

Before you overtake you must:
- Wind your nearside window down in order to bark low abuse at the driver you wish to pass.
- Shout 'Get out of the way, you geriatric incompetent arsehole.'
- Be sure that the driver of the vehicle in front is made aware of your intentions by aggressively weaving from side to side like a drunken stunt car from *The Dukes of Hazzard*.
- Flash your lights, sound your horn and generally seethe in a sociopathic manner.
- Turn up the volume of a qualifying cock-rock anthem and salute the memory of **MARC BOLAN.**

While overtaking
It is often necessary to deploy psychological techniques in order to stamp your authority over lesser drivers. There are two approaches: Antagonistic, where you laugh like a maniac and show them your shotgun; and Relaxed, where you take the opportunity to catch up on some light flower arranging, that novel you've been trying to finish or perhaps choosing some new wallpaper.

If you are being overtaken
- **Do not take it personally.** Your energies would be better channelled into researching cures for your erectile dysfunction or pondering why all the men you meet are wankers.
- **Steer a straight course** and avoid throwing a milk bottle of urine at the passing car.
- **Look straight ahead.** Do not make eye contact with the other driver, even if you have an interest in shotguns or wallpaper.

Creative overtaking

Permissible if the driver ahead is adhering to the speed limit, creative overtaking is one of the many techniques you will need to master in order to start collecting penalty points.

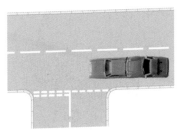 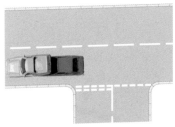

The up and over. If there is no let-up in the stream of oncoming traffic you will need to mount the vehicle ahead in the manner of a **RUTTING BISON.** Hit the booster switch located on the underside of your seat, next to the piece of last summer's chewing gum, and drive your vehicle on to the roof of the car ahead.

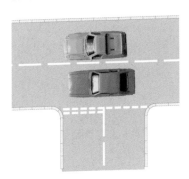 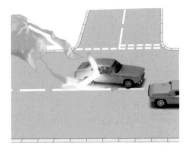

The Molotov cocktail. Sometimes overtaking can simply not convey the sheer frustration inflicted by being stuck behind the driver of a 1970s Capri. In such cases throw a Molotov cocktail through the driver's window as you pass to remove them completely from this mortal coil.

Driving in adverse conditions

Weather

Driving in extreme weather conditions can be alarming, especially if you can't see where you are going and end up floating towards an oil tanker in the English Channel.

106. Here are guidelines for driving in the following conditions:

Rain Turn on your windscreen wipers. Drive faster and take the opportunity to soak pedestrians by aiming for puddles beside the pavements. It is, strictly speaking, illegal but they will:

• not have time to get your number plate down;

• be far too ashamed to go to a police station;

• get depressed. Depressed people don't see the point in complaining. Rain is also useful for washing your car if you don't know what a shammy leather is.

Fog Turn on your fog lights. Imagine you are flying through a cloud. Speed up from time to time to see how courageous you are while driving without knowing what's ahead. *The Myway Code* advises that flirting with death is a good way of keeping alert on long journeys.

Sun Put on sunglasses, wind down your windows and put some R&B on your stereo. Then look beautiful pedestrians up and down with a perverted look on your face before smiling suggestively at anyone that gives you eye contact.

WARNING: Be careful not to contract White Van Man Arm during the summer months. White Van Man Arm is so named after the tan line that forms across the right arms of White Van Men from their shoulders down to their sovereign-ring-clad fingers. No one would dare take the piss out of such White Van Man markings on the beach of resorts like Falaraki in Greece, where they form part of the bizarre mating rituals that pass for courtship between the White Van Men and maidens of Britain's North Easterly towns. Outside of this context they are grounds for withering middle-class ridicule.

 Snow Tighten every muscle in your body, hunch your shoulders, suck air in through your teeth, grip your steering wheel so tightly that your knuckles go white, and wince in anticipation of a disastrous crash.

You'll probably be fine, but following this procedure will ensure that the minute you step out of your car you'll slip over and splinter your coccyx.

107. Of course, weather is just one of the adverse conditions you may sometimes find yourself driving in. You may also find yourself having to contend with the following distractions:

- Driving with a map-reader who doesn't know where you are.
- Driving with someone who won't shut up.
- Driving while children quarrel in the back.
- Driving in the process of arranging a divorce.
- Driving with a passenger who has just passed their test.

It is the last of these that is of the greatest concern. The others can all be avoided, by purchasing a **SAT NAV** system, earmuffs, a highly strung Alsatian and a bunch of flowers respectively. But there is nothing you can do that will repair the damage to your soul caused by sharing your car with a newly qualified driver. You will be able to tell if your passenger has just passed their test by looking out for the following tell-tale signs:

- **They will bang** on the dashboard with their hands when you drive over any sleeping policemen to give the impression that you are not giving them a comfortable ride.
- **When you approach** a stationary vehicle at a normal speed they will wince, push their right foot forward as if to brake and then complain that you are travelling too fast.

- **They will hold** on to the handle above the passenger side door when you take a corner at a suitably exciting speed, before exclaiming, 'Jesus Christ that was close.' When it clearly was not.
- **They will say,** 'According to the Highway Code you should travel in the left-hand lane at all times where possible, so strictly speaking, because we are outside the hours of its operation, you should now enter the bus lane.'
- **They will offer to drive** even though they know you'd far rather have your genitalia deep-fried while they are attached to your body than risk death by being *their* passenger.
- **They will tell you which lane** they think you should be in as you approach a roundabout and 'tut' if you enter a box junction.
- **Give you a running commentary** whenever you park detailing exactly at what point they would have turned towards the pavement when they would have locked the steering wheel at exactly what speed they would have attempted the manoeuvre when you should straighten up.
- **It is also likely** that they will gibber and cry when you slam the boot shut on their interfering, obnoxious little faces for the remainder of your journey.

Really extreme driving conditions

The Myway Code advises that you must never drive during:
- Typhoons.
- Hurricanes.
- Glacial meltdown.
- Interplanetary collision or the death of a nearby red dwarf or similar collapsing star system, where pole reversal may adversely affect the circulatory direction of mini-roundabouts.
- Armageddon.
- *Top Gear* presented by His Holiness the Great Clarkson and that ubiquitous little git who presents it with him, you know, the one unable to say 'No' whenever anyone offers him the chance to front a

crap book, television programme or media engagement of any kind.

108. Driving when carrying murderous passengers

In the event that one of your passengers should attempt to strangle you with a coat hanger it may be advisable to vacate your vehicle while you are still moving.

- Simply direct the car towards the nearest cliff/wall.
- Press hard on the accelerator.
- Unclip your seatbelt.
- Open your door.
- Roll out onto the road protecting your head with your hands. Your assailant will curse the day he decided to attack you up until the point of impact.

Evasive driving techniques

Even though the East and West have now settled their differences, it is inevitable that, at some point during your driving life, you will find yourself being followed by a renegade member of Stalin's Politburo through a snowy forest. You can prevent anything nasty happening to you and your family by adopting these simple security measures:

- **Change your vehicle regularly.** Keep a spare car in secluded woodland at all times, allowing you the chance to switch vehicles if you feel suspicious about the man following you to your local swimming baths in a Vauxhall Viva.

- **Use false identities** when dining in a Little Chef or staying in a Travelodge. Having alternative names and cover stories (legends) for you and your children will put most would-be assassins off your scent.
- **Have** grenade launchers installed the next time you go for an MOT.

- **Always make sure** that your front cannons are fully loaded. You'll find the magazine just behind the windscreen wash fluid.
- **Participating service stations** stock ammunition behind the pasties in the chill cabinet. In an emergency, however, a Cornish pasty fired at close range can do substantial damage.
- **Use alternative routes to the supermarket.** Double-backing and driving in a completely different direction for three hours should shake off any agent on your tail.
- **Devise a code word** to notify your associates that something untoward is going on while loading your vehicle in the car park of a nearby DIY Super Centre.
- **When arguing** with your associates about directions remember they are not your real partner, just another intricate aspect of your legend.
- **Cover the floor** of your garage with a layer of **TOMATOES** so you can instantly tell if an intruder has been tampering with your vehicle while you are asleep.

Strategies for dealing with the world we live in may include installing a fully grown tigress in your rear seat.

- **Install** a fully grown female tiger in the rear seat of your car to prevent hijackers taking you by surprise.
- **DO NOT** rely on in-car GPS systems to inform you about incoming missiles. Use your mirrors.

If these basic prevention techniques do not deter your attacker then you will have to perform exciting manoeuvres while under machine-gun fire:

- Handbrake turns
- J-turns
- U-turns

In an emergency **ALWAYS** remember, Mirror, Signal, Ejector seat.

Did you know?

- **Captain Death** is available to hire for all sorts of non-death-related celebrations. An improvement in car safety features (airbags, seatbelts, traffic congestion that has reduced the average road speed in Britain to 20 mph), has forced Death to diversify into other areas of commerce. So if you want Captain Death to appear as a surprise guest at your granny's ninetieth birthday party contact *The Myway Code* HQ.

Waiting and parking

109. Double yellow lines are specifically designed to give you a nasty feeling. They are not yellow by accident. We wanted them to have the same effect on cars that wasps have on people, hence the wasp marking. Nobody wants to sit on a wasp so, by tapping into the same intuitive wariness of things with yellow and black markings, we ensured that no one would want their car to sit on them either. This is evidence of the mastery of psychological knowledge at work within *The Myway Code*. We spent a fortune on a behavioural therapist to come up with that. Yours is not to reason why. We know what we're doing. We're messing with your mind all the time.

Parking

110. When you have arrived at your destination you will need to park your car unless you immediately want to drive back home again. Parking is, therefore, quite useful. Parking spaces beside roads are becoming an endangered species however, leading some motorists to just stop their cars and park in the middle of the road.

The more affluent the area you are driving in the more disdain you will notice from drivers when it comes to parking regulations. This is because fines only deter people who can't afford to pay them. Rich people like footballers, MPs and the bored and botoxed wives of businessmen living in **KNIGHTSBRIDGE** think of parking fines as just a form of legalized bribery. They don't have to give a toss about whether or not you can park somewhere because they think traffic wardens are valet parking attendants.

111. In the unlikely event that you find somewhere where you can legally park:

- **Stop nice and close to the kerb** but be careful not to scratch your alloy wheels.
- **Turn off** the ignition.

- **Apply** the handbrake.
- **Cry** with joy at your good fortune.
- **Alight** from your vehicle.
- **Take one last look** at your scratch-free paintwork.

112. You MUST NOT PARK in the following places:
- **Widthways** across a lane on a dual carriageway.
- **On a Zebra crossing** (although it is permissible to park on an **EVIL TWIN ZEBRA,** see p. 10 for more information on exorcising the Evil Curse of the Great Zebrada in the event that you cross an **EVIL TWIN ZEBRA** crossing).
- A bus lane, cycle lane, or anywhere it would be really useful.
- In London.

113. Parking Permit Only signs

The procedure required for actually getting your hands on one of these is so irritating, miserable and frustrating that it far outweighs the benefit of actually having one.

To acquire a parking permit you'll first have to go into a crack-addled part of town and try and hold a conversation through an inch-thick glass barrier on account of the violent, drugged-up tax-dodgers that frequent all council-run establishments. Then there's the multitude of identification documents you have to take with you, along with your council tax bill and a letter excusing you from PE written by your mother when you were twelve. In the unlikely event that you are allowed to buy a permit you'll then have to travel six and a half miles to another council office to actually pay for the bloody thing.

114. Road markings. The Myway Code (Draconian Provisions) Act of 2006 has introduced the following road markings, restrictions and penalties to Britain's highways:

- **Green lines.** You may only park on green lines to purchase organic goods, a sprout and bindweed vegetarian pasty or an edition of *Sanctimonious Eco-Git Monthly*. Unfortunately, your ecological principles may authorize traffic wardens to tow away your car and recycle it into sandals on environmental grounds.

- **Purple lines.** Analogous to standard yellow lines in depressed provincial towns where all the Goths drive hearses. Parking is restricted to the duration of 'Lucretia My Reflection' by the Sisters of Mercy.

- **Transparent lines.** A new class of parking restriction that puts the onus of deciding whether or not parking is permitted onto camouflaged parking attendants cunningly disguised as free parking notices.

- **Triple yellow lines.** No parking, waiting, stopping, slowing down or discussion, cogitation or theorizing about parking, waiting, or slowing down is allowed along triple lines, establishing the UK's first traffic thought crime.

- **Silver lines.** In certain Royal Boroughs, planning requirements stipulate that the colour of road markings must not adversely affect the character of the neighbourhood or otherwise lead to the impression that the residents are, in any way, common or poor.

115. Parking meters offer a way for motorists to pay for exactly how much on-street parking they may require by dividing the hour, then the minute, into infinitely tiny chargeable segments. In today's time-sensitive world, with hand-held computer scheduling and strict productivity targets, modern parking nano-meters can measure lengths of time shorter than the duration of a wasp's breath.

Parking nano-meter durations

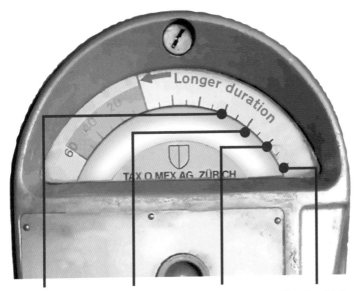

Average duration of a humming-bird fart.

The anti-corrosion warranty of an Italian car.

The approximate length of a wasp's breath.

The time it takes to really dislike a new employer.

116. Goods vehicles often have to deliver things to shops so that we can buy them. But in London they are not allowed to park within a mile of the shops they need to deliver their goods to because of the congestion charge. This charge is about to be raised to £1,000 per day in order to prevent anyone actually living in London annoying the city's tourists. London is not designed to be lived in, it is a crime-ridden theme park existing purely to fleece Americans and trivialize the Queen.

117. Parking at night. You are far less likely to get caught bashing into another car when parking at night.

118. Parallel parking. Successfully performing a parallel park between two vehicles feels fantastic. The nearest a non-driver can get to understanding the sense of achievement attained when performing this manoeuvre is when you unload one of those rare behemoth stools that you don't have to strain to remove and which leaves the merest patch of moisture when you wipe yourself afterwards.

119. Parking on hills. Off-road vehicles create exciting opportunities for drivers. The countryside has become like the Internet for cars. Now you can drive everywhere. When parking your off-road vehicle (ORV) be careful not to crush walkers and ramblers (WAR) although scaring them by pretending you are about to can be great fun.

Parallel parking guide

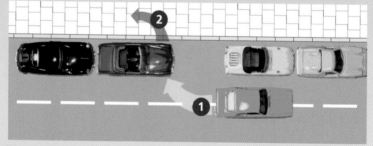

1 **In tight spots,** it may be necessary to encourage other cars out of the way. This applies particularly to cabriolets and other convertibles favoured by the financially well-endowed. Reverse onto the offside wing of the car to the rear of your intended parking position.

120. Reverse parking. When you learn to reverse park you never have to do it within the vicinity of another vehicle. Consequently when you have passed your driving test you will find yourself completely unprepared to for the reality of reverse parking in any instance when it is actually required. This is all part of the driving instructor's bizarre teaching ritual, which is designed to create new drivers who are fully qualified to drive in empty car parks but be completely hopeless on actual roads.

121. DO NOT park your vehicle or trailer in the following places:
- Outside an Accident and Emergency Department.
- Across a railway crossing.
- In a school swimming pool.
- On a sandbank at low tide.
- On a zigzag bend.
- On a humpback bridge.
- Outside the weekly meeting of the *I don't have any common sense because I'm a sodding moron* support group.

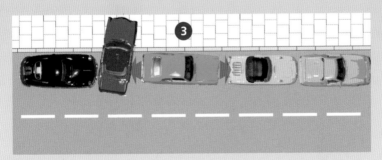

2 **Gently push** obstructing vehicle onto footway, watching out for pedestrians and the potential owners of bourgeois automobiles who can be identified by the trail of bemused ordinary folk in their wake.

3 **Exert forward and aft pressure** to cars. Walk quickly away.

Motorway driving

General regulations

Many other rules apply to motorway driving. Listing them here would simply be too tedious for words.

122. Motorways are a special class of road where vehicles are required to continuously accelerate until there is an accident of some kind.

123. There are two main kinds of motorway. The first kind is the standard, purpose-built variety – a neo-brutalist expressway ploughing headlong into a future populated by androids flying aircars and devising societies loosely based on the Roman Empire, but with an intellectually interesting substratum of 21st-century intolerance and authoritarianism. These motorways are usually allocated an M number – e.g. M1, M2, etc. The 'M' stands for 'Modern'.

The second type of motorway is assigned a normal road number, followed by an M in parentheses – e.g. A394(M). These motorway-class roads are the result of local councils' conversion of one or more existing A-class roads, cycle lanes, towpaths, public bridleways, etc. into a coherent purposeful-looking road to make their town seem busy and metropolitan in road atlases. This has the effect of drawing in more investment bankers, venture capitalists and restaurateurs. Most motorway-class road systems are, therefore, ultimately a way of finding a nicer place to have lunch.

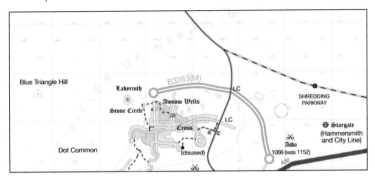

124. The eventual aim of motorway driving is to travel at the speed of light and create temporal paradoxes that will **JUSTIFY** the enormous cost of building the road in the first place, thereby silencing all critics of roads and branding them as the enemies of progress and science. For these reasons, they are not suitable for use by:

- **Herds** of cattle.
- **Morris Minors or 2CVs,** where insoluable time paradoxes – those of rustic, bucolic simplicity and a relaxed attitude to the passage of the seasons – will cancel out the awesome effects of travelling by motorway.

125. Certain other roadusers are forbidden to use motorways either on the grounds of safety or because the Ministry judges them not fashionable enough to match its svelte and streamlined view of the future. They include bicycles, prams and pushchairs, mopeds, carriages for the

differently-abled motion-impaired, lawnmowers under 500cc without a grass collection box, **JAPANESE SEWING MACHINES** and all trams incapable of running without a lengthy extension lead.

126. At motorway speeds, reaction times are critical and alertness is absolutely paramount. For instance: when travelling at 1,800 mph in the middle lane of the M4, it can take the full length of the Maidenhead bypass in order to complete a satisfactory yawn. You must therefore look further ahead than on any other road and develop some form of extrasensory perception, such as clairvoyance or, after a short seance and the provision of a notepad and pencil, automatic writing, before setting out on your journey. There are now many advanced schools of motoring which offer basic and intermediate courses in remote viewing and other forms of ESP. Details are already in the post to you, following your perusal of this paragraph.

127. Driving at velocities in excess of Mach 1 will mean that other road users may not perceive you until the sound of your V-24 Bastard quad-turbo has arrived at the corpse-littered trail of devastation you are now safely miles ahead of.

128. Before you start your journey **YOU MUST** make sure that you are alert enough to use the motorway. Signs that you are not 100% in command of your reactions and focussed on your journey include:
• **Joining the M1** with your slippers on.
• **Joining the M1** with your slippers on.
• **Reading** the same paragraph twice.
• **Sipping a malted barley hot drink,** pulling up the duvet, turning the headlights out and saying goodnight to your passengers.

129. Before you join the motorway, you should ensure that your car is not only safe enough to travel at high speed, but is also able to weave around the road in an alarming and possibly threatening fashion. There is no better time to perform last-minute vehicle checks than at the last minute, so pull over on the slip road and carry out the following essential inspections:

- **Radio.** Motorway journeys are so long and tiresome, it is not possible to complete one without listening to local radio stations along the route. Local radio performs a vital function on motorways because it fills the vehicle cabin with such tedious, dreary drivel, phone-in after pointless phone-in, that everything outside the car suddenly seems life-affirming, exciting and worth taking note of.

- **Tyres.** Make sure that you have tyres, that they are inflated and they are all mounted on wheels. Furthermore, make sure that the wheels are mounted on your car. *The Myway Code* recommends that you carry one spare tyre in your boot and four or five in the back seat of your car. SUV drivers **MAY NOT** carry one 'safari-style' on their tailgate, unless they agree to be mauled by a lion every 10,000 miles.

- **Brakes.** If you are unable to stop on the slip road because of poorly functioning brakes you will not be able to stop to test your brakes to find out whether they are defective or not. Either way, you are now speeding down the motorway with defective brakes and you're reading a book. It's all a bit worrying, isn't it? We should have probably mentioned this earlier. This book cannot help you, so you should put it down now and concentrate on – and endeavour to make plans for – the rest of your life which, at the very least, shouldn't take you very long all of a sudden. Maybe you should do something exciting with it, or maybe you've had enough of excitement right now.

Joining the motorway

You normally join the motorway via an acceleration lane or slip road. Some motorways may additionally provide an elastic catapulting device or a series of skate park-style ramps and half-pipes to boost acceleration and to facilitate execution of advanced driving manoeuvres.

130. Motorwetiquette. Because motorways are the highest rank of the Queen's Highway, custom requires you to perform the following **LAST-MINUTE CHECKS** as you reach the end of the acceleration lane to join the flow of traffic:

- **Use your offside wing mirror** to straighten your tie.
- **Remove your hat and scarf** and hand them to your houseboy, manservant or butler.
- **As you approach the end of the slip road,** beg leave to join the motorway. If refused, you must reverse up the slip road with your headlights dipped and your head bowed. It is a matter of regal etiquette that you should not look directly at the motorway.

Using the motorway

131. Know your lanes. Newly qualified drivers often make the mistake of referring to the three lanes of a standard motorway as the slow, the middle and the fast lanes. This is a fallacy. All of them are fast.

132. You must NEVER stop. From a strictly **LEGAL** standpoint, you are forbidden to stop your vehicle anywhere or at any time while driving on a motorway. This has a number of consequences for delayed traffic, which may be forced to drive slowly around in circles until the blockage is cleared. Longer tailbacks can lead to huge synchronized wheeling and turning displays, similar to the aerial manoeuvres of autumnal starlings.

Motorway service areas

133. In keeping with the futuristic style of Britain's motorways, service areas are provided in which motorists may eat, drink tea-like or equivalent quasi-drinks and relax in a low-rise glass and steel building designed in the style of an interstellar space station or the Central Atrium from the popular TV series *Logan's Run.*

Architect's drawing of the proposed *Mercy Dash* service area that skilfully avoids including any visual reference either to the 100-foot-wide environmental disaster that it serves or to the aura of suicide-grade ennui that hangs over the whole bloody enterprise.

These space-age constructions are made up of a series of areas linked by neon-illuminated hallways decorated in a manner that promotes creeping apathy, followed in time by overwhelming desperation.

By their very nature, service areas are full of people who would rather be almost anywhere else, and it is for reasons of customer empathy that they are staffed by people who have no wish to be there either.

A typical service area, such as the proposed *Mercy Dash Services (above)* to be run by *Bonjour Cuisine,* comprises the following:
- **A 24-hour restaurant** serving food that is both warm and soft enough to fall asleep in.
- **A shop** that sells super-scale paperback road atlases detailed enough to map the country at one inch to the yard, while physically large enough to block out all light from the sun.

- **An amusement arcade** frequented by straw-sucking psychopaths who are worryingly proficient at gun-based games.
- **A large wet room public convenience,** where customers are free to simply piss on the floor.
- **A coin-operated business card printing machine** perfect for midnight changes of identity while on the run from the police.
- **A preternaturally empty car park,** given the 600-strong queue of people at every facility in the service area.
- **A motoring organization salesperson** who will not let you join if you actually need to.
- **A gang of local youths** in a souped-up Morris Marina powered by a tractor engine and sporting an in-car stereo so powerful it is not allowed to be switched on within 100 metres of a Grade 1 listed building.
- **A petrol station** staffed by the terminally unwilling.
- **A motel** that was converted from a 1980s college of further education, and is manned by staff that were headhunted from the O Level Tourism and Recreational Studies course.

Local services

134. Local services are for motorists in an advanced state of pelvis-busting urinary longing who find themselves on a motorway or primary route where there are no official services. To access local services:
- **Take the turning off** the motorway where it says 'local services'.
- **Pass the over-cultivated** and frankly daft floral roundabout which spells out the name of the village in pansies.
- **Drive three miles** down a potholed, bladder-bashing road.
- **Park** in the abandoned car park with the most definitively closed toilet block since someone filled a urinal with concrete in the name of art.
- **Dream** of your ideal slash-stop – some kind of unisex drive-in urinal where you could simply park and let go as you waggled into neutral and let the clutch out.
- **Piss** yourself.

Independent roadside service stations

135. Found in laybys alongside impoverished daffodil sellers and broken glass, the independent roadside service station is frequented by lonely truckers, women in their fifties with bad skin and people on the run from the law.

Characteristics of the independent service station include:
- 'Service' from an unfathomably enormous man called Bill whose level of personal hygiene can only be described as 'relaxed'.
- No attractive branding or textural lighting of any kind.
- Knives and forks chained to the table.
- No spoons.
- Alfresco bathroom facilities.

Did you know?
- **If all of Britain's motorways** were laid end to end, the M25 would have to be sliced into and prised apart to facilitate straightening.
- **All of Britain's motorway service** areas will one day group together to form an autonomous federation that will rule the Earth.
- **Junction 7 of the M1** is Britain's oldest motorway junction. An Iron Age slip road on the site was discovered in 1988 during the excavation of Verulamium Roman Services on Watling Street(M).

CAPTAIN DEATH SAYS...

Breakdowns and accidents

136. If your vehicle breaks down you will know because it will have stopped moving and/or smoke will be billowing from under the bonnet.

In the event of a breakdown you should leap around behind your vehicle shouting and screaming to let passing motorists know that you are experiencing problems.

If you have an emergency reflective triangle **THROW IT** at the first car that refuses to stop to help. Alternatively, hammer some nails into it to turn it into a DIY 'stinger' stopping device to force a passing motorist to come to your aid.

It is possible, at this juncture, to descend into a complete **NERVOUS BREAKDOWN** as an overpowering sensation of helplessness and loss fragments your spirit and you collapse under the realization that in life you are, really, completely alone. Stranded, if you will, in an inexorable existential vortex for which a roadside breakdown is the perfect metaphor.

If you feel that an act of suicide would perhaps overstate the seriousness of breaking down you may find the following five-point breakdown procedure helpful:
- **Shout** 'Fuck' continuously.
- **Pound** the steering wheel with your fists.
- **Cry.**
- **Become disproportionately paranoid** about the threat of being attacked while you sit alone on the hard shoulder.
- **Wait several hours for a man in a boiler suit** to take you to a garage where a friendly mechanic will show you a lump of scrap

metal before convincing you that it is your broken driveshaft and charge you £900 plus VAT to fix it.

If it is night and visibility is poor, **STAR JUMP** across the road into the path of oncoming traffic – someone is bound to stop and help you. Even if only to prise your left kneecap out of their radiator three hundred yards further down the road.

Additional rules for the motorway

While driving on a motorway, if your vehicle starts to judder in a frightening manner, a whining noise develops or sparks follow the rear of your car no matter how much you swerve across the road to evade them, then your vehicle may be about to break down. In which case **VEER WILDLY TO THE LEFT** and deposit your vehicle on the hard shoulder. If the car is stolen, this is a good moment to scale the bank beside the motorway and leg it into the closest available woodland.

If it is your vehicle then you must not run off into the closest available woodland. You must take responsibility for the ostrich-like attitude you have displayed to your clearly dilapidated and under-appreciated Freedom Wagon. Now you know the pain of the pedestrian. Take more care of your vehicle in future: without it you are **TRULY IMPOTENT.**

Simple repairs may be carried out on the hard shoulder. Keep tinfoil (to spark and jump-start your battery), a belt (to re-attach hanging exhaust pipes) and a spotlight (to blind passing motorists to force them to stop and help you) in your vehicle at all times.

Children can be entertained by winding the lone country and western cassette tape in your glove box around a nearby tree. Adding enough wow and flutter to country and western tapes to make the whining and twanging indistinguishable from the distortion is both a fun game and a service to music.

If you are unable to repair your vehicle by reading the Haynes Manual and applying rudimentary knowledge of the internal combustion engine then **YOU ARE A LOSER**. You will need to arrange roadside assistance for which you will quite rightly be overcharged.

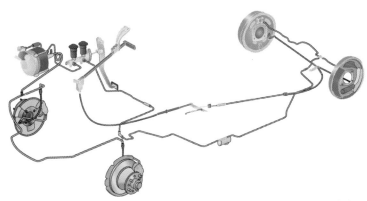

If your car looks like this when you get it back from its annual service, it's likely that your mechanic is having a serious nervous breakdown and has an enormous bag of spares at his disposal.

If you feel at risk from another person while waiting to be rescued you should curse yourself for not getting round to learning a martial art at any point in the previous ten years. By now you could easily have been a black belt or yokozuna and would be able to take any would-be attacker with ease.

IF YOU DO GET ATTACKED you may like to use the following quote from the celebrated film *Withnail and I*: 'I've got cancer, if you hit me it's murder.' Roadside attackers have seldom seen it, and will be unaware that you are both a) defending yourself with great cunning and b) making a hilarious reference to an excellent movie.

In the event that you are not afraid of being attacked, stand well back from the hard shoulder while you wait for assistance.

137. Before returning to the carriageway after a breakdown you will need to accelerate wildly. If there is no room on the motorway then hammer your horn and shout, 'Get out of the fucking way' before swerving back onto the road as aggressively as possible. To achieve the required level of anger just look at the bill you were given by the roadside mechanic.

138. If you are unable to move your broken-down vehicle onto the hard shoulder you are completely fucked. Remember, real drivers go down with their cars.

139. Obstructions. If any item falls from your vehicle on the motorway, stop and retrieve it only if it can be traced back to you.

Disabled drivers

140. If your disability prevents you from following the advice above then don't worry about it. You've got this far on your own so you must be pretty resourceful.

WORK COMMENCES

On these pages at some point in the future.

We apologize for any inconvenience.

Railways and level crossings

Other rules apply to railways, in particular, regulations stipulating that you should not eat the sandwiches and should only buy the tea if all your supplies of battery acid have been exhausted.

141. Level crossings occur at intersections of the road network and the rail 'system'. They usually consist of some kind of automatic gate mechanism which closes the road so that trains can pass. This mechanism usually includes warning lights that flash in advance of a train approaching. The sequence is as follows.

- **Amber light flashing and an audible warning.** You are very lucky. This means that a Train Operating Company (TOC) has managed to safely pilot a train for long enough to initiate an OSAE (On Schedule Arrival Event) at a series of stations between the point of departure along the DRS (Decrepit Railway System) to where you are now. You will be able to tell your grandchildren that you actually witnessed a train during the Great Age of the TOCs.
- **Red lights begin flashing.** You are in luck. After about 20 minutes of humming along to the audible warning, letting your mind construct riffs out of the insistent doo-de-deh-doh until you come up with your own Kraftwerk tune, a train may soon appear. In years to come, you can tell your grandchildren of this event. However, disappointment is still possible at this point.

What to do if you get stuck

- If you get caught on a level crossing, you may find everything goes uncannily quiet at first.
- You will notice that the world around becomes grainy and black and white, following which a manic piano starts playing and twenty-five policemen arrive in the back of an open-topped Model T Ford and start running around doing slapstick with ladders.
- Your situation will not be their first priority if there is already a lady tied to the tracks nearby.

 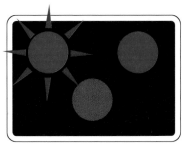

After a train has passed, you can tell if another one is on its way by the audible sighing of everyone present.

- **The barriers go up.** If the train did not pass, it is possible it has suffered an EDE (Engine Disappointment Event) which may have been exacerbated by a lightning strike by members of the Union of Signalmen, Engineers, Loafers, Electricians and Sleeping Station-masters. The only people working on the railways are now the Administrative Unit Who Think Up Acronyms (ARSEHOLES) in order to appear dynamic and modern, while striving to offset the continual sense of Rail-Based Disappointment (RBD).

This is what a level crossing usually looks like – signals, gates, white picket fences, the lot, but no actual trains on account of them all being broken.

Tramways

In addition to the rules in the following section, people interested in driving trams should grow a handlebar moustache, buy a pair of breeches, be fascinated by mundane local history books and explore the wilder realms of personal hygiene.

Trams. Why? This is the latest model, apparently.

142. Trams originated during the Victorian era and are an amalgamation of the great technologies of that time – the squeezebox accordion, the commercial biscuit tin, electricity and the chin-length sideburn.

143. If you are driving down an ordinary city street and suddenly find yourself in the path of an oncoming runaway train, chances are that you are about to crash into the most bothersome part of a modern metro system – the tram. Either that or you have unwittingly slipped through a wormhole into the early 20th century. Look around for the presence of grinding inner-city poverty, feral gangs of ragamuffins and paedophiliac peers of the realm, to assure yourself that you are, indeed, still safely in the 21st century.

144. Because they are old and out of date, most drivers haven't got a clue how to deal with these oversized biscuit tins that refuse to die. Are they just trains that have been let loose on the roads? Can they steer or not? Everything about trams is stupid, from the annoying whine they make when they move to the idiotic 'tramline' hairstyle they inspired.

145. Tramlines and cyclists. Tramlines, however, are useful for teenagers on bikes. Ride between the tramlines and it's like having your very own oversized Scalextric track to ride along. They can be dangerous though, but then that just adds to the fun.

146. Tram signals. Trams have their own signs and signals that look like liquorice allsorts, there's no need for them to be different. It's just an attempt to make them seem mysterious and interesting. But even being in Bond films has failed to do that.

How to drive a tram

Trams are very simple to drive but first you must follow the correct health and safety procedures:

- Wear a tank-top.
- Grow a beard.
- Develop an uncontrollable twitch.
- Cultivate a collection of warts on your left arm.
- Dirt-ify your fingernails.

It is also advisable to stand up while you are driving a tram or 'on the handles' (as it is known to the lonely men with strange bouffant hairstyles known as tram enthusiasts). This is not to give you a better view of the traffic ahead, but to prevent you from falling asleep due to the unparalleled tedium of travelling in one of these strange contraptions.

Light signals controlling traffic

Traffic lights use subconcious psychological colour cues to control the flow of traffic at busy interchanges. Red appears closer than other colours, green means far horizons and amber is the colour of flux and ambition, subject to the provisions of the *Road Traffic Act (Incandescent Bulbs Order), 1988*.

Where used in conjunction with **HOLISTIC, CHESS** and **GO CLASS BOX JUNCTIONS** *(see pp51–53, paragraphs 96–99)*, traffic lights

Signal sequence

Red means STOP. You may take this chance in your driving day to relax, unwind a little and take it easy. **RED** means you can change radio station, put on a CD or rev your engine therapeutically. Or, if you have disruptive children or a troublesome, meddling partner, **RED** also gives you a few moments to lay down the law, start an argument or raise a controversial point that cannot be fully investigated or challenged before the amber signal appears. This is the way of **RED.**

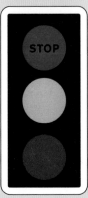

Red and amber still means stop. AMBER signals instil a sense of anticipation in drivers, cut short any arguments initiated during the red phase and let passengers know that they may not distract your attention any further, no matter how urgent or pressing the matter may seem to them. AMBER tells them that you are about to resume the paramount business of driving, as a result of which, everyone and everything else is by definition wrong. This is the way of AMBER.

embody many of the key teachings of Eastern philosophy and are regarded as oracular means of divination in their own right.

As with most aspects of *The Myway Code* and other occult philosophies, traffic light divination becomes a matter of **INTERPRETATION.** Most students of *The Signals,* however, prefer to consult the *I-Ching* – in particular, the constructs embodied in hexagrams 36 through to 40, from 'brightening of the light', through 'obstruction' and on to 'disentanglement'.

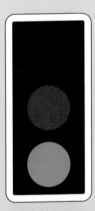

Green means GO. The balance of your driving life has been restored fully after the interruption of red and amber and you may proceed, subject to qualification from extra signals *(below)*, on your way, safe in the knowledge that red signals are holding back other traffic.

Go in peace, my child. This is the way of GREEN.

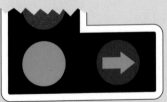 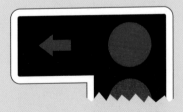

Qualifying traffic signals. A green arrow to the right *(left)* means oncoming traffic has been obstructed to make your chosen path clear. The oracle says: 'Do not feel sad for oncoming traffic, it is but a gnat's cough until it resumes. A fallen tree lets the light in.' A red arrow to your left *(right)* may mean your colour vision has been affected as a consequence of your car rolling over. Check for a pink sky where the ground usually is.

What your car says about you

People will judge you by the car you drive. It's as simple as that. So you must choose your vehicle wisely.

Ferrari, Bentley, Rolls-Royce, Jaguar, Aston Martin, Daimler

Driving is the only time you ever have to mix with ordinary people who have to work for a living and cook their own food. You frequently write to your friends in the House of Lords to enquire when 'Celebrity and Rich People Only' roads will be built. Until then you must endure the odious world of the hoi-polloi.

Maserati, Lotus, Lamborghini, Mitsubishi Lancer Evos

A car was the first proper relationship you ever really had. You would rather wax it at the weekend than cover your partner in baby oil. These vehicles are also popular with men who enjoy taking their sister's boyfriends out for a spin through country lanes at Mach 12 – well, you've got to liven them up a bit haven't you?

Land Rover, Hummer, Chelsea Tractor, Jeep

You're selfish and not quite as rich as you think you are. You chose a car that would elevate you from other road users and justify it because it is safer for your passengers. The fact that these cars kill more children than the Israeli Defence Force and the Palestinian Liberation Organisation combined is lost on you completely. Because you know you'll be dead by the time the ice caps have melted you don't care about the environment either. Spearmint Rhino's anyone?

BMW, Audi, Alfa Romeo, Mercedes, Saab

You can't quite understand why anyone would spend over £20k on a car and not buy one of these brands. You have to be able to afford one of these cars by the time you reach a certain age or everyone around you will regard your life as a dismal failure. *(Note: Convertible BMWs are now only ever driven by nineteen-year-old estate agents.)*

Mondeo, Lancia

You drive for a living. You buy your suits in Suits Etc and use Regain in an attempt to stem the tide of ageing. You spend many hours trying to work out whether wearing a Simpson's tie makes you look cool or not, but you didn't think twice about buying a Mondeo/Lancia. Or we're talking about your dad, and because he's got company insurance he lets you, his seventeen-year-old son, drive it to college every now and then. He has no idea how many times you have nearly died while racing your mates down the local dual carriageway.

Fiesta, Fiat, Citroën, Honda, Daewoo, Hyundai, Renault, Vauxhall

You've never really understood the concept of choosing a car. They just seem to appear when you need them. You came to own it by accident, someone gave it to you or you were offered it cheap. You can't understand why people get excited about the car they drive. You much prefer watching reruns of obscure science fiction television shows, compiling parodies of government guidebooks and sounding off about politics in the pub.

2CVs, bubble cars, Robin Reliants

You have dyed your dreadlocks red and live in Brighton. You've taken

quite a lot of mind-altering drugs. You turned your back on mainstream society because you simply couldn't hack it. Now you're into chanting and sticking pins in yourself in an attempt to make yourself seem interesting.

Pontiac, Chevrolet, Chrysler, Cadillac, De Lorean

You still hold the view that became popular around the time of Huey

Lewis and the News, circa 1980, that America and all things American are cool. They aren't. You love the fact that most people are under the impression that these cars cost as much as Ferraris. They don't.

Volvo

Volvo drivers are split into two dreary categories. You are either a timid sandal wearer that still hasn't come to terms

with the fact that nine people die on the roads every day so you have to drive round in a breeze block. Or you are a completely insane motorist that crashes all the time and has to drive one for your own protection.

Rover

You didn't? No seriously, you didn't buy a bloody Rover? Well now

you're completely buggered. They are slow, staggeringly uncool, and you won't be able to get any spare parts when it inevitably breaks down. You are a fool, or an unlicensed taxi driver.

Signals to other road users

According to *The Myway Code*, smoking is naughty and wrong and unspeakably filthy. Some drivers, however, find those three inches of high-visibility fire stick a semiological extension to their malodorous nicotine-stained fingers and may use the following cigarette-brandishing signals for emphasis:

- **I am very relaxed** and will shortly execute a beautiful right-hand turn across three lanes of traffic using only one hand, both my knees and a certain level of suave derring-do. *Malheureusement*, I am French and do all of this from the wrong side of the road.

- **I am about to turn left** and will withdraw my cigarette so that it does not counteract or negate the effect of my left-hand indicator – the passenger who is smoking in the nearside seat on my behalf and has badly singed the fascist health-fanatic cyclist I have just cut up.

- **I have dropped a lit cigarette** into my lap and my trousers may well be on fire. While I am busy scrabbling around in my seat and screaming, please pass on either side and call the fire brigade.

- **I have just suffered** a major heart attack and/or pulmonary embolism, brought about by my dedicated services and support of the nicotine-industrial complex over the years. For the purposes of *The Myway Code*, my car may now be classified as a temporary bollard. Please pass on. I know I have.

Signs and signals

Introduction

There are approximately 3 million signs on Britain's roads of which
there are four categories: warnings, orders, information and direction.
You may find all of this terribly interesting, but wait until we tell you
about the subcategories and start mentioning different colours and
shapes – trust us: you'll be completely blown away.

Red signs

Triangular
Warning

Circular
Prohibition

Star of Pentacles
Word of The Beast

Blue signs

Rectangular
Information

Circular
Mandatory instruction

Blue Cross
Sale at Debenhams

Direction signs

Blue
Motorway

Green
Primary route

Cardboard
Farm shop

Warnings, orders and instructions

Warning signs

Jesus!

Saviour ahead

Fu@k!

Something dangerous
yet unspecific

Dunno

Your guess is as
good as ours

**Middle
England
ahead**

Stuck-up Cassandras

**Giant
raptor
looming**

Capture possible

Footnotes*

*Conditions apply

Alien
cattle mutilation

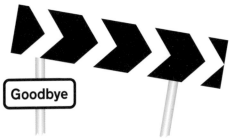

Goodbye

Calamitous deviation over cliff

Warning signs (continued)

Sky

Maximum height
of atmosphere

LloydsTSB

Prowling bank
call-centre staff

**For 2
Fathoms**

Naval flotilla
crossing ahead

**If you're
scared**

**Swerve
around**

**1970s
playground
ahead**

**4 wheels good,
2 wheels bad**

**Determined
suicide attempt**

**Pontiff
crossing**

Signs giving instructions and orders

Anarchy

Cycle path mounted on top of bus

The Answer

Screwdriver required

Chinless inbred buffoons approaching in centre of road

Enormous garage bill in the offing

Exactly

You must not deviate from 120 mph

Road rage: Queensberry rules

Christian youth club meeting

Information signs

Information signs, which are all rectangular, aim to enrich the driving experience by giving supplementary information to road users.

Priority to confident traffic

Go on, tough it out

POLICE STATE

PLEASE LINE UP AGAINST

THE WALL QUIETLY

A sign of things to come

You really shouldn't read every word on this sign.

By the time you've read down to here you will have travelled over two hundred yards without watching the road.

If you're still reading it now then you are about to crash.

Well we did try and warn you.

Do not read this sign

STOP!

THIS INCONGRUOUS

TRAVEL

INTERCHANGE

RESTRICTION IS

ACTIVATED FOR

MAMELUKES* ONLY

Roadside word puzzle

Nosy neighbours
and suburban
vigilante zone

Secluded scenic
spot for suicide

Smile!
Nobody likes a
grouchy speeder

THIS IS NOT
A ROAD

These signs are positioned off the public highway, alerting drivers of Chelsea
tractors that they are as unwelcome here as anywhere else

Self-explanatory signs not explained

YOU SHOULD HAVE LEFT **MUCH** EARLIER

WELL WHAT DID YOU EXPECT? IT IS THE **RUSH** HOUR

THERE'S NO USE GETTING **ANGRY** ABOUT IT NOW

YOU WON'T GET ANY SYMPATHY FROM ME, ESPECIALLY IF YOU'RE **MAD** ENOUGH TO HAVE A CONVERSATION WITH A SIGN

Placename signs

HULL
'It smells of death'

Sizewell
Mind how you glow

You are welcome to

Bradford

'Not as bad as the statistics might suggest'

A404

This village
cannot be found

You are now entering

CORNWALL

'Everything is further away than you expect'

Welcome to *Here*

Twinned with
There & Everywhere

Britain in Bloom regional loser 1978

KENTISH TOWN

'Where tramps go to die'

North Sea
•OCEAN DRIVE•
Sorry about the smell!

Port Talbot
'It's really bad, even for Wales'

St Andrews
FAT AMERICAN GOLF WIDOWS WELCOME

Please drive carefully through the village

MIDDLESBROUGH
Football colours only

PORTSMOUTH
'The home of facial tattoos'

Tourism signs

Following consultations with the tourism industry, tourist signs were introduced in the 1990s to help motorists find their way to attractions. In recognition of the environmental impact of many tourist attractions however, directions appear on a poo-coloured sign. A selection is shown below.

Jane Austen's World of Tedium →

↑ A waste of your money

Desk Fan Adventure Park 300 yds

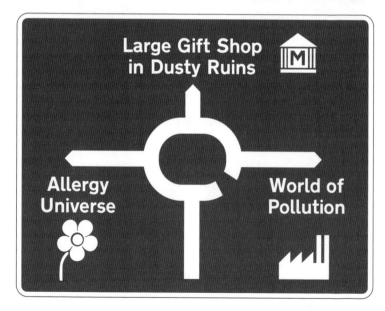

Large Gift Shop in Dusty Ruins

Allergy Universe

World of Pollution

£10 to go 100 yards in an anorak →

 Graffitied stones in an isolated field →

← **A house Charles Dickens once walked past**

 *i* **Tourist Information**

Special tourist information boards are sometimes situated in lonely parking spots and laybys and advertise a broad range of local activities and attractions where visitors to the area may be assured of a friendly welcome.

Motorway signs

Direction signs

Motorway direction signs are the size and colour of a three-storey house that has been painted blue with white lettering on it.

You're better off on the motorway, really

Public service announcement

Throw your mobile phone out of the nearside window before the cops catch you

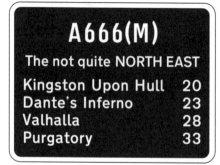

Route confirmation sign

Motorway broken

Regulatory signs

There are many rules governing motorway use, see pages 72–79 as we really can't be repeating ourselves. We are the government and you will do as you're told. It's for your own good.

Light signals on motorways

Because of the tremendous speed of motorway traffic, signs must always be succinct and easily comprehensible like this one, which simply urges you to stop whatever it is that you're doing as it is bound to be wrong in some way.

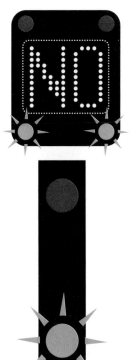

Signals on crap motorways

Some motorways are not as swish and fabby as others because, inevitably, in the provinces they are grateful for what they get.

On these motorways, you may notice one of these signals. It means that 'an unspecified hazard is occurring at some point or another.' Often this is simply a school crossing patrol or a herd of Friesians drifting across the carriageway in dense fog and there's nothing to worry about until you start hearing a series of dull thuds.

A statement from the Department of Political Correctness

At an enormous and utterly pointless cost to the taxpayer, versions of all these signs are also available in Braille.

Motorway services signs

A blue background with white lettering and icons, with optional air rifle pellets and buckshot texturing.

Services

M5	DELUDED CHEF	1m
M6	BONJOUR CUISINE	20m
M42	CHAVELLER'S REST	24m

Distances to next dumps

You don't really have any other choice, do you?

Petrol 699 p

Rip-off confirmation sign

Services icons

Fast food restaurant

Overpriced fuel on sale

Customer service award

Pedestrian direction signs

Like motorway signs, pedestrian signs feature blue backgrounds with white lettering. Which explains why ramblers sometimes run around the motorway trying to overtake Lamborghinis doing 80.

Where's he off to?

Primary route signs

Primary route signs have green backgrounds and white lettering, with road numbers marked in Smiley Sunshine Aci-i-i-i-i-d Yellow.

New trunk road signing

Route confirmation

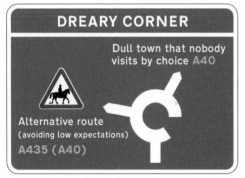

Super-descriptive advance sign

'Interesting' junction ahead

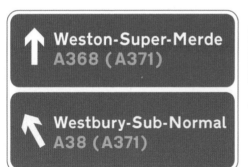

Sign featuring local slang town names

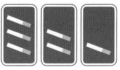

'Countdown' markers, showing the distance to the start of the junction's slip road. Each diagonal cigarette represents approximately one full, deeply satisfying drag

Roadworks and diversion signs

MAJOR ROADWORKS

Delays inevitable until the end of time

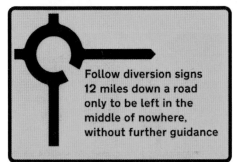

Follow diversion signs
12 miles down a road
only to be left in the
middle of nowhere,
without further guidance

ACCIDENT AHEAD

A motorway maintenance lorry has shed its load of traffic cones, leading to the creation of 50 temporary lanes

1-1″
33 cm

Road traffic cones have numerous functions on Britain's highways, but are chiefly used to mark an obstruction on the road caused by the placement of the cone itself. Individual cones may also be used to mark out parking spots outside your front door, as impromptu megaphones or hats for town centre sculptures of tiresome people from the past.

Deep road trenches must be marked by flashing beacons at night, pursuant to Section 17 of the Large Holes in the Ground Act, 1954. However, a gaping hole in the Large Holes in the Ground Act itself means that they may also be taken home to adorn the bedrooms of teenage boys with insufficient access to disco lights. The lights will blink slowly for a number of weeks, reinforcing the sheer dreadfulness of any miserable teenager's music collection.

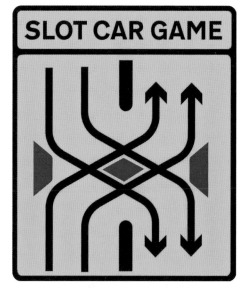

A blatant attempt to be controversial

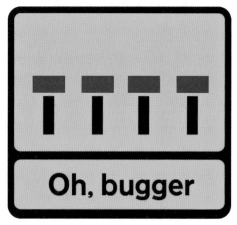

The T shape stands for toast, which is what you will be if you do not slow down

Experimental junction layouts

The Myway Code introduces new junction layouts from time to time to experiment with traffic flows and ease congestion where possible. The nature of modern road use, however, is so complex and chaotic that the *Code* is to introduce new point-scoring systems to junctions to calculate who has right of way at any particular point. The first of these systems is to be used at the new so-called Wimbledon junctions.

The new so-called Wimbledon junctions

Wimbledon junctions are based on the rules and regulations of the Lawn Tennis Association, along with those of the popular card game *Top Trumps*. Each driver scores points based on their levels of aggression and skill at the junction, as well as key features of their vehicle, such as acceleration or top speed. The points are then all played out on road markings based on those of a tennis court. A match umpire adjudicates from the top of a converted traffic light pole.

Where there are filter lanes or a dual carriageway involved at the junction, rules for a doubles match come into play and the tramlines may be used.

Where there are actual tramlines, incorporating real trams, the junction reverts to singles-only operation and drivers will be asked to 'play a let' by the umpire.

'Sue Barker' writes:
- In the example opposite, the yellow Lancia looked a bit rusty as it went out onto court, but soon gained the upper hand based on its *Top Trumps* score for acceleration. It has now approached the net to win the game from its already commanding 40–30 lead.
- The VW puts in a fine performance with a couple of great rallies, including one in Newquay with 2,000 other camper vans.
- The Mini Cooper could not win from this position, purely on account of it being British.

How the points stack up

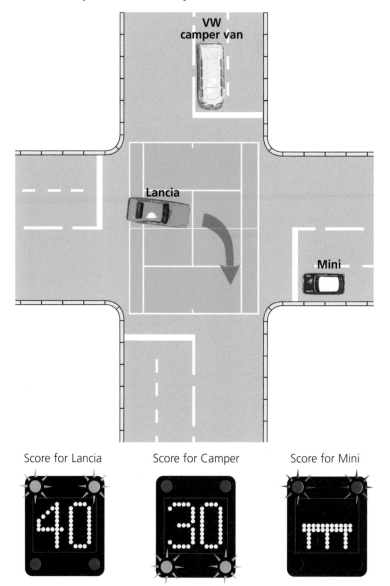

Score for Lancia

Score for Camper

Score for Mini

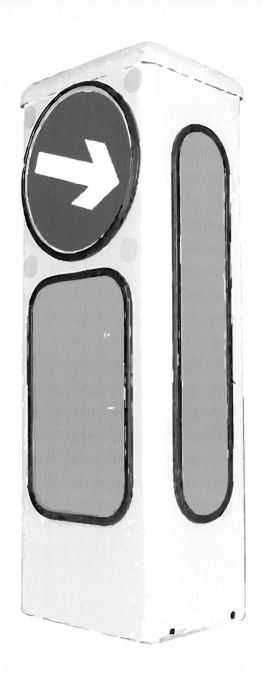

Annexes

1. The dashboard

Modern cars are powered by onboard computer systems many times more sophisticated than even Orac used in *Blake's 7*. Unlike Orac, however, modern engine management systems cannot communicate with all other computers – their poor networking capabilites are one of the main reasons given for the lack of interest shown in these powerful computers by bounty hunters working on behalf of the Terran Federation.

Newly qualified drivers – having learnt to drive in a no-frills vehicle that is mostly reliant on radio valve technology – may be confused by all this enhanced engineering, where some of the familiar buttons have changed their function and new controls have replaced some of the old.

Hazard warning indicators. The onboard computer uses a complex algorithm – based on your driving patterns and a voice recognition circuit that can detect spoken abuse from other drivers – to determine whether or not it should send a team of software welder-bots down the circuit to fuse the switch in the 'on' position permanently or simply swerve you into the kerb in the interests of general road safety.

The horn. The largest and, arguably, the most important button in the car. Where once a simple hooter parp would suffice, today's aurally literate road users only respond to the latest digitally enhanced sounds – such as the **RIDE OF THE VALKYRIES** as rendered by small-arms fire or the voices of neuro-linguistic programming experts that can persuade anyone who cuts you up to drive to the foot of the nearest cliff, via the top of the nearest cliff. All of which are downloadable from specialist road ragetones websites.

The box junction ejector seat control panel. Only to be used where the infinitely complex rules of box junctions become so taxing you are no longer able to complete your manoeuvre. **WARNING:** Ensure sunroof is sufficiently open before deployment.

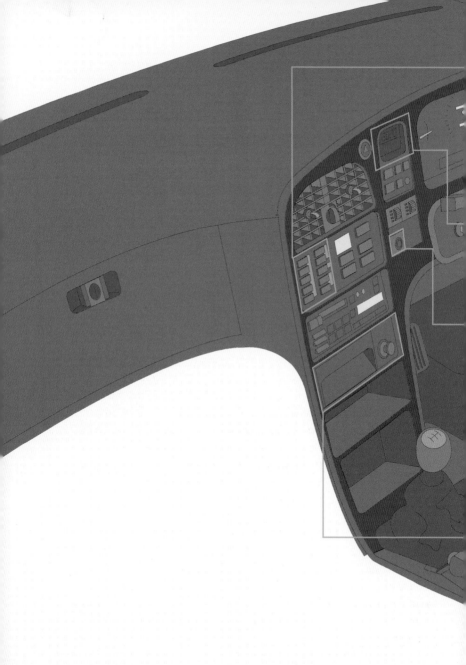

Windows buttons. Handy shortcut keys for re-booting the car in case of software configuration errors that can occur from time to time. If you find the sunroof opens when you indicate left or that you can perform stunning handbrake turns by dipping your headlights, this button will either enable you to execute a soft restart or it will unexpectedly deploy all the airbags and engage reverse gear. **NOTE:** To avoid the Windscreen of Death, you should press this button from the back seat using a long twig.

LED display. Not just a clock, but a multi-purpose unit that can display the time in six different time zones, estimate the number of cat's eyes you have passed, show your GPS location and calculate the overall *Top Trumps* score of your car at any point in time.

Start button. The touch-sensitive circuit controlling the start function in modern automobiles has replaced the simple key-operated on-off switch of yesteryear, opening a whole new world of possibilities. By measuring the force applied to the button and then taking readings from the sweat on your fingertip and comparing them with ambient humidity and temperature levels for instance, the start button can assess your mood before it lets you begin your journey. Half-hour tracks of calming music and joss stick **SCENT** simulation counteract stress, while positive reinforcement messages play when you feel out of control or inadequate in any way. Just what you need when you are late for that extremely important meeting.

Addiction system helper. Not just a cigar lighter, but a portal to an entire new world of hands-free chemically induced wonder and glory, the ASH tray is like an air-conditioning unit and tobacconist rolled into one. Now that holding anything in your hand is illegal while driving, the ASH tray immerses you in an atmosphere of pleasure by pumping your preferred stimulants into the air automatically.

2. The way of the White Van Man

To drive a white van is the pinnacle of driving achievement. White Van Men drive with such a high degree of confidence, mere mortals must assume they have discovered the secrets of eternal life, such is their flagrant disregard for all aspects of road safety.

In a rare interview with one of their code (who risked permanent expulsion from their number for divulging the furtive mysteries usually only handed down through a complex ritual involving a tanned right arm and putrid pies), published here for the first time, in writing, are the clandestine procedures of the noble and mysterious White Van Man.

Rule 1: The divine right of the white van
The road-using infrastructure depends on a class system where your vehicle is king. No vehicle is more royal than the white van. Here is the natural order of things:

White Van Man – Only the Gods know why White Van Men move in such mysterious ways. They drive more than all other road users and have acquired knowledge of the road the like of which you can never hope to achieve. No one will tell you you are ready to become a White Van Man. If you are ready, you will know.

Black/Yellow**/**Orange**/**Green**/Blue/Brown Van Men.** This is the sequence of coloured vans you must drive through before being assigned your White Van Man status. You must show deference to all other road users throughout this period of humility and education.

Lorry drivers – Rather like retired Jedi masters, White Van Men will bow to their wisdom and experience but know that their time on the road is coming to an end.

Bicycles – Fearless warriors. Like luminous ninja they prey on the souls of all drivers. Do they not fear death?

Motorcycles, cars, disabled wagons, roadkill and horses – Road detritus.

Rule 2: Thou shalt cut up all road users

Because of the sheer number of vehicles using the roads they require self-policing. It is the duty of all White Van Men to uphold the **CODE OF THE ROAD**, through the infliction of the fabled cut-up ritual, wherever a lack of respect, according to the Divine Right of the White Van Man, occurs.

On the high street

If any vehicle cuts you up on the high street then pause for a moment. This will lull them into the belief that you are not about to act with damning precision.

THRASH your engine fiercely before pulling away into a controlled wheel spin (never mind the fact that you will seemingly have to stop in stationary traffic ten yards further up the road). This act of bravado will render your opponent speechless and unable to hold your gaze as you pull out alongside them, causing all oncoming traffic to come to a halt. **THE FOOL**! Imagine thinking that you, as a WVM, are bound by the trivialities of road law that they stick to like frightened children! A traffic jam is nothing to you!

Remain motionless, staring intently in their eyes as their attention flickers between your nightmarish gaze and the **ATTRACTIVE YOUNG LADY** featured on the cover of the *Daily Star* you have placed, exactly for that purpose, between your windscreen and dashboard.

Remain still and stare at your foe's confused visage. Within seconds they will give way and wave you ahead, chastened and shaking, thanks to the adrenalin tsunami now coursing through their veins.

They will not bother you again.

On the motorway
Any madman prepared to take you on the motorway is a treacherous foe indeed and must be dealt with by a new kind of tactical terror that requires ungoverned use of all available lanes on the road.

Start by driving at just under 70 miles per hour. This will flush out any cocky drivers with ideas above their station.

Allow yourself to be overtaken and laugh manically as another plaything stumbles into view. Let them gather speed and move on ahead. This gives you time to suss out your foe as they sit, feeling smug and self-satisfied, doing 75 miles per hour in the middle lane.

Now the balletic manoeuvre of the motorway cut-up can begin.

Start by driving alongside the **IMBECILIC WORM** on their left-hand side as though you intend to undertake. This will unsettle them at once, especially if you remain there for some time. Their confidence will waver and crumble as they begin to realize the enormity of their error. **THE FOOL**! For thinking you are bound by the trivialities of orthodox road law and not allowed to overtake in whichever lane you like! But you will not overtake. Not now, not yet.

Just as they begin to slow down to move behind you, then you slow down also. Easy now. Easy.

COME INTO MY WEB SAID THE SPIDER TO THE FLY.

Your assailant is now yours to play with. Play as you will.

To conclude the procedure slow down so the front of your van is parallel with the back of their vehicle and then, exhibiting the outright mastery of your profession, overtake them so fast and so savagely that they are convinced you shaved their back bumper as you swept behind them into the outside lane.

Now for the mortal blow.

Go to overtake **BUT DO NOT.** Instead, sit parallel to them in the outside lane, staring enraged and shaking your fists as the last remnants of their courage dwindle. Under no circumstances accelerate to overtake. Instead allow them to glide back behind you, vanquished, where they belong.

If you have carried off this manoeuvre perfectly you will spot your assailant in your rearview mirror, weaving around in confusion before exiting the motorway at the next available service station for a cup of sweet tea.

Amen.

3. Penalties

There's only one person worth asking about penalties and that's **SOUTHAMPTON FC'S** footballing genius, Matthew Le Tissier. He only missed one out of fifty in his career and he missed that one on purpose because he was bored and felt sorry for Nottingham Forest's Mark Crossley.

According to our research, after watching clips of Le Tissier in action, this is how to score a penalty.

1. **Don't take too long a run-up** or you'll fall over and **LOVEJOY** the ball over the bar.

2. **Keep your head down over the ball,** otherwise you'll look like a right wally and spoon it up into the terraces.

3. **Leather it hard into the corner.** Even if the keeper dives the correct way, if you've hit it **HARD** enough he won't reach it.

4. **Practise.** And according to Le Tissier, 'Try to put as much pressure on yourself as you can. I used to take penalties in training against the youth team goalkeeper and offer him money if he saved them. Knowing how desperate he was – he was only on about £50 a week – I knew he'd try his best.'

Getting penalty points on your driving licence
Whether or not you get points for driving depends on whether you get caught breaking driving regulations. How many points you have on your licence says a lot about what kind of driver you are. See the summary opposite to see how you stack up:

0 points

You drive like a right wimp. You never go over the speed limit or have any fun. You don't like getting excited in case you wet yourself. You've probably had some of those green 'P' plates on your car for the last three years.

1–3 points

You got done for speeding once and felt weely, weely bad about it. You have furry toys hanging from your rearview mirror and you're not being ironic.

4–7 points

You are a proper driver. You've got the right mix between flirting with danger to impress the people around you and knowing the score about actual road safety. If you didn't have a satellite speed-camera detector on your dashboard you'd have been banned years ago, but keeping one step ahead of the authorities is just the kind of person you are.

8–11 points

Easy tiger. The life of the pedestrian awaits if you carry on ignoring those speed cameras.

12 points

Oh dear. You'd better go and buy some *Reebok Classics.*

(Note: If **NQD**s get six points on their licence within two years of passing their test then they have to go back to driving around empty car parks with blokes in beige cardigans who like to talk about how impressive their lives are when they're not teaching people how to drive.)

4. *The Myway Code* Store

There are many ways to express your continued interest in *The Myway Code* through the act of pointlessly spending money. The following pages feature crap promotional trinkets that somehow relate to the *Code* that we thought up last night in the pub to satisfy insatiable consumer demand.

This sign has been ignored, abused and mistreated, but you can send it a message of love and hope.

Adopt a road sign, and in return we will send you a Welcome Pack, containing: a photograph of your sign in situ, a personalized adoption certificate, a cuddly version of your sign, facts about your adopted sign, a greetings card on your birthday from your sign, and tips on how you can continue to hand over bundles of your hard-earned cash to people desperate to exploit your gullibility. You will also receive quarterly updates about your sign's progress in *Road Sign Owners Magazine*.

The money you pay goes towards the repainting and general upkeep of your sign. Your sign will also bear a silver plaque detailing your name so complete strangers can marvel at your generosity.

> **'He who hath want of a guiding light can come unto me and crosseth to the other side'**
> *The Myway Code* **(King James Authorized Version, 1611)**

Meticulously crafted in the finest porcelain and featuring a flashing head, the guardian of all Zebra crossings is celebrated in this attractive figurine which will soon become the talking point of your home. This stunning portrayal in porcelain (also available in adjustable flesh-coloured vinyl) captures the pontiff in an elegant pose, with arms outstretched welcoming drivers and pedestrians alike.

- Hand-numbered limited edition of only 750,000 worldwide.
- Approximately 16 inches in height.
- Place your order now!
- Also available as a twin-pack gift set, incorporating crossing stripes and short length of road. Approximate dimensions: 20 x 50 feet.

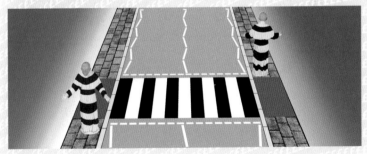

- **NOTE:** Buying a porcelain pope will not guarantee a place in heaven, although it may well increase your likelihood of entering hell.

Own a strip of hallowed tarmac

Buy your own slice of the M25 to re-lay in your drive (also available in a presentation case). Recreate the magic and wonder of the largest city bypass in the world outside your own home by re-laying this hallowed piece of tarmac in your driveway. Only £45 for one square foot or £90 if you require a piece with painted road markings.

Just imagine, this lovingly crafted, high-quality original M25 surfacing can be yours to own outside your own home.

Road layout towels for the man who has everything

The ideal gift for that special man you can't be arsed to choose a proper present for at Christmas. Available in any layout you care to mention, cycle lanes, blank tarmac, junctions, slip roads … oh for God's sake, why don't you just put £20 in the bin?

Beat congestion and ease domestic traffic flow with *Myway Code* road markings and layout features for the home

This new deep shag pile carpet decorated with various classic road markings can help point out who has right of way in the home. Identical in every respect to real road layouts featured up and down the UK and made famous in this book.

Every product comes with an authoritative guide on how to enforce the Road Traffic Act in your own home.

Box junction: Ideal for outside the bathroom if you have teenage children.

Primary routes: Avoid painful collisions to and from the kitchen with these primary route signs which will enable you to start your very own domestic route network.

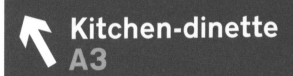

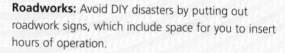

LOUNGE WALL RESURFACING

Work commences 16 April and will continue until Mum decides to hire someone professional

Roadworks: Avoid DIY disasters by putting out roadwork signs, which include space for you to insert hours of operation.

Cones for the home: Our new fabric road cones are ideal for advising guests that hoovering and dusting is about to commence.

Roundabout port dispenser: A decanter and turntable arrangement that moves only to the left.

Hours of endless road fun and games dressed as Captain Death

You can now find popular road safety superhero **Captain Death** in your own home. The Captain Death Suit is available in adult and children's sizes for fancy dress and Halloween parties. **NOTE:** Scythe, cloak and skeletal frame not included.

What if I haven't found something I like in *The Myway Code* store?

We can sell you anything with *The Myway Code* logo on it: If we have been unable to think of enough rubbish for you to spend your money on then please call *Myway Code* HQ and we will be happy to arrange for our logo to be applied to any old bit of tat you like. **Price on application.**

Delivery Options

Money-burning Courier Service

NEW

Why wait four days for your purchase when you could get it in three and a half? Pay our convenience tax of £60 per item, which includes insurance cover (and peace of mind) in the event that an oversized marigold falls on you and your purchase at the precise moment of delivery.

Platinum Insurance Price Plan

If you're the kind of person that finds it more satisfying and enjoyable to pay over the odds for everything you buy simply because it makes you feel more successful, then the Platinum Insurance Price Plan is for you. Add an extra 20% to the final total of your bill for no discernible benefit whatsoever and we will make sure that the delivery man pretends he thinks you are a celebrity.

5. *The Myway Code* theory test

Introduction

Your theory test will take place in an unmarked Seventies building identifiable by the amount of people feverishly smoking on the pavement outside it. You will need to take your passport, provisional driving licence and a letter from your mum explaining that you haven't ingested any cough mixture during the previous twenty-four hours.

You will then be led into a booth containing a touch-screen personal computer by a friendly, plump woman wearing glasses like Ronnie Corbett's. She will tell you to relax and to take your time when answering the questions.

You will need to answer thirty questions correctly out of a possible thirty-five. Thirty-three will be so easy only a frozen lobster could get them wrong, the other two are so obscure you will only know them if you have read *The Myway Code* fifty times on account of it being the fiftieth time you have taken the test because you have the intelligence of a frozen lobster. Once you have answered all the questions check them over once but then leave it or you'll start to get paranoid and change correct answers into incorrect ones.

After that you will be led into a dark room for the final part of your theory exam, the Hazard Perception Test. This involves having large pieces of road furniture thrown at you from behind a counter by a large unfriendly man in a duffel coat. You will be expected to evade significant injury as well as to give a comprehensive description of each sign, bench and safety barrier hurled in your direction, in the order it was thrown, once the klaxon sounds.

Alertness

01   Before jumpstarting your car in a thunderstorm with a sparking overhead power cable: **SELECT ONE ANSWER**

☐ **a)**   Wash your hands.
☐ **b)**   Check your hazard warning lights are on.
☐ **c)**   Write a will.
☐ **d)**   Come to your senses.

02 When following a driver displaying a 'baby on board' sign in their rear windscreen: **SELECT ONE ANSWER**

☐ **a)** Look in your wallet/purse to reminisce over pictures of your own children.

☐ **b)** Stop your car, exit your vehicle and halt all traffic behind you. Then inform all other road users that the car ahead has an 'ickle baby' in their back seat and that its parents would like everyone to turn their radios down.

☐ **c)** Crash into it regardless of what the sign says.

☐ **d)** Decide, having seen the sign, not to run them off the road into the next available ditch.

03 Your mobile rings on the back seat while you are doing 130 mph on the outside lane of a motorway. You should: **SELECT ONE ANSWER**

☐ **a)** Stop immediately exactly where you are. Driving while a phone rings can cause accidents.

☐ **b)** Answer it, tell whoever it is you are driving and cannot talk for long in case you get nicked, and then hang up.

☐ **c)** Pull over at the nearest suitable place.

☐ **d)** Unpack your hands-free kit and plug one end of it in your phone and shout 'Hello?' over and over again with increasing volume, then give up and throw it all into the back seat.

04 In which of the following occasions would you never overtake a man in a shopping trolley: **SELECT TWO ANSWERS**

☐ **a)** While he's floating in a canal.

☐ **b)** When you are also in a shopping trolley.

☐ **c)** When you are on a blind corner.

☐ **d)** In the crisps and snacks aisle.

05 You approach a set of traffic lights, which have been green for some time. You should: **SELECT ONE ANSWER**

☐ **a)** Maintain your speed.

☐ **b)** Accelerate fiercely.

☐ **c)** Close your eyes and accelerate fiercely.

☐ **d)** 'Egg and chips please.'

Attitude

06 Tailgating means: **SELECT TWO ANSWERS**

- [ ] **a)** Reversing into a gate to gain unauthorized access to a field.
- [ ] **b)** You are in a rush.
- [ ] **c)** Driving backwards down the motorway.
- [ ] **d)** 'Bigamy' in Azerbaijan.

07 You should not wave pedestrians across the road in front of you while driving because: **SELECT ONE ANSWER**

- [ ] **a)** It may upset the delicate equilibrium of the highway if you allow them to get ideas above their station.
- [ ] **b)** They might think you're going to run them over.
- [ ] **c)** They may produce a squeegy and wipe grit and dirt across your windscreen.
- [ ] **d)** They might not actually want to cross the road.

08 What should you use your horn for? **SELECT ONE ANSWER**

- [ ] **a)** 'Fnaar fnaar.'
- [ ] **b)** 'Ooo, you are awful.'
- [ ] **c)** Signalling.
- [ ] **d)** To convey extreme agitation.

09 You are driving along a country road and come across a young woman on a horse. You should: **SELECT TWO ANSWERS**

- [ ] **a)** Select 'Killing in the name of' by Rage Against the Machine on your stereo, turn the sound up to eleven and open your windows to notify her of your presence.
- [ ] **b)** Drive past slowly and give her plenty of room.
- [ ] **c)** Approach slowly and at the last minute veer wildly into her path so the horse ejects her into a thorny hedge. Then muse idly on how much pain the world would have been saved had someone done that to Trinny or Susannah when they were lording it around Hampshire on the back of a stallion forty-five years ago.
- [ ] **d)** Use your horn, flash your lights and rev your engine to keep her on her toes.
- [ ] **e)** Select 'The Imperial March' from your *Star Wars Greatest Moments* CD, turn the sound up to eleven and open your windows to notify her of your presence.

10 You are driving down a long and winding road at night. You should: **SELECT ONE ANSWER**

- [ ] **a)** Look out for venison you can sell to a local butcher.
- [ ] **b)** Turn your lights off to see what driving by the light of the moon feels like.
- [ ] **c)** Hum 'The Long and Winding Road' by Paul McCartney.
- [ ] **d)** Pull over and hunt for faeries.

Safety and your vehicle:

11 Which of the following should you check before setting out on a long journey? **SELECT ONE ANSWER**

- [ ] **a)** The number of wheels on your vehicle.
- [ ] **b)** Your email.
- [ ] **c)** That you have a length of rope, some canned food and a loaded shotgun in your boot in case of civil unrest or nuclear war.
- [ ] **d)** The levels of dilithium crystals in your proton drive.

12 If your tyres are under-inflated, what is likely to happen? **SELECT ONE ANSWER**

- [ ] **a)** You may feel slightly depressed while driving.
- [ ] **b)** You will find it harder to wheel-spin and lose self-esteem as a result.
- [ ] **c)** You will no longer be able to see over hedges in the countryside.
- [ ] **d)** Your tyres will wear unevenly and you will have to stop every 5 miles to turn them inside-out to compensate.

13 If your vehicle begins to judder violently you should: **SELECT ONE ANSWER**

- [ ] **a)** Pull over and carefully dispose of any bottles of nitroglycerine in your boot.
- [ ] **b)** Take the opportunity to make a martini-based cocktail you can be really proud of.
- [ ] **c)** Stop driving backwards and forwards over that cattle grid.
- [ ] **d)** Not buy any more cars manufactured by Zanussi or Hotpoint or any other brand that promises fuel efficiency on urban and spin cycles.

14 Name **ONE** reason to fit a roof rack to your car.

- [ ] **a)** Go on, I bet you can't.
- [ ] **b)** A constant nagging whistle as I am driving helps me to become agitated with my ungrateful family, causing heated arguments which, therefore, promotes a climate of quiet fear that helps me concentrate on the road.
- [ ] **c)** It's somewhere to strap the children to after the climate of quiet fear wears off.
- [ ] **d)** Because I am pathetic.

15 Which of the following environmental statements is true? **SELECT ONE ANSWER**

☐ **a)** A car uses less fuel on an urban cycle because it only uses two wheels and never stops at traffic lights.

☐ **b)** Biodiesel is made from decomposing oil company executives.

☐ **c)** Electric cars will never become popular until that joke about extension leads is told another four billion times.

☐ **d)** Even a journey of a thousand miles starts with a single step – usually off public transport and straight into a car.

Hazard awareness

16 Another driver's actions cause you to feel angry. You should: **SELECT FOUR POSSIBLE ANSWERS**

☐ **a)** Shout abusive language.

☐ **b)** Reach for the weapon you have concealed beneath your seat.

☐ **c)** Follow them home while flashing your lights continuously.

☐ **d)** Overtake them to assess their size and build before taking steps to escalate the situation into a physical confrontation.

17 You have just left hospital while bleeding and wearing a white robe. Before you drive you should: **SELECT ONE ANSWER**

☐ **a)** Check you are not drifting in and out of consciousness.

☐ **b)** Locate your car.

☐ **c)** Turn the heater on.

☐ **d)** Remove the drip still in your right arm.

18 You have taken illegal drugs, and have the urge to drive home. You should: **SELECT ONE ANSWER**

☐ **a)** Laugh in that strange, manic way that people do when they've taken drugs.

☐ **b)** Ascertain whether or not you are hallucinating.

☐ **c)** Ring a government helpline.

☐ **d)** Smoke a few more joints to calm yourself down and proceed to your nearest Hob-Nob shop in order to giggle like an infant.

19   A motorway journey is tedious. You should: **SELECT ONE ANSWER**

- ☐ **a)** Veer about wildly to inject some excitement into your journey.
- ☐ **b)** Open your window and attempt to hold a conversation with the driver of the car beside you.
- ☐ **c)** Practise juggling.
- ☐ **d)** Embark on a fondue.

20   Which **TWO** result from drinking alcohol:

- ☐ **a)** Fun.
- ☐ **b)** Sex.
- ☐ **c)** Laughter.
- ☐ **d)** Becoming a gangster's bitch in prison.

Vulnerable road users:

21   You are driving behind an elderly driver. You should: **SELECT ONE ANSWER**

- ☐ **a)** Get out of your car and overtake them on foot to make a satirical point.
- ☐ **b)** Follow them home to make sure that they are wrapped up well, their living room is not full of newspapers from the 1950s and their chest freezer does not contain their partner who mysteriously disappeared in 1987.
- ☐ **c)** Rev your engine aggressively to simulate the sound of a doodlebug.
- ☐ **d)** Sit in their passenger seat and look for Werther's Originals in their glove box.

22   Which road users are especially in danger of not being seen as you reverse around a corner? **SELECT ONE ANSWER**

- ☐ **a)** People who have the power of invisibility.
- ☐ **b)** Ghosts.
- ☐ **c)** Motorcyclists wearing special chameleon jackets that dynamically change colour to blend into the background.
- ☐ **d)** Spies in stealth gabardine suits.

23   A wheelchair user is waiting to cross at a Zebra crossing. What should you do? **SELECT ONE ANSWER**

- ☐ **a)** Wave cheerily as you pass them – it brightens their blighted life and there's nothing a disabled person likes more than being treated as if they were normal.
- ☐ **b)** Drive around the back of their chair and push it across the road with your car.
- ☐ **c)** Stop and ask them to sign your copy of *A Brief History of Time*.
- ☐ **d)** Tell them that you have seen *Reach for the Sky* and therefore understand them.

24 What do the road markings above mean? **SELECT ONE ANSWER**

- [ ] **a)** You are about to pass a school playground and should watch out for an enormous slick of marbles in the road.
- [ ] **b)** There is a danger of seeing a corduroy jacket and/or elbow patches soon – do not be alarmed by their sense of fashion.
- [ ] **c)** You are a worried parent in an SUV and this is your parking spot.
- [ ] **d)** Beware of incoming stink-bombs.

25 Roughly how much extra room should you allow when overtaking a horse? **SELECT ONE ANSWER**

- [ ] **a)** It depends on the racecourse.
- [ ] **b)** You're the experts, you tell me.
- [ ] **c)** Enough room to ensure the stirrups do not scratch your paintwork.
- [ ] **d)** One furlong.

Other types of vehicle

26 It is raining. A motorcycle approaches on your side of the road at great speed. You should: **SELECT ONE ANSWER**

- [ ] **a)** Close your eyes and say three Hail Mary's.
- [ ] **b)** Momentarily reflect that driving a 4x4 at this juncture was a good idea. He'll bounce off you like a fly.
- [ ] **c)** Slow down and pull over.
- [ ] **d)** Perform a U-turn to escape whatever is chasing him.

27 The bus in front of you stops to pick up passengers. What should you do? **SELECT TWO ANSWERS**

- [ ] **a)** Pull out and overtake on principle.
- [ ] **b)** Watch out for stupid poor people crossing the road in front of you.
- [ ] **c)** Wait for it to signal and continue its journey.
- [ ] **d)** Pull out and overtake on principle.

28 Outside are four cars. Which one is yours? **SELECT ONE ANSWER**

- [ ] **a)** None of them, but I borrowed the Fiesta from my gran.
- [ ] **b)** The Capri that matches my outfit.

c) You'll have to ask my chauffeur.

d) The manure-powered tie-dyed tricycle. I don't agree with cars. By the way is this the right building for the 'cooking with cardboard' evening class?

29 The road is wet, busy, and it is hard to see because of the spray coming from the caravan in front of you. You should: **SELECT TWO ANSWERS**

a) No it isn't. After much deliberation I didn't go out in my car because driving in the rain is so dangerous.

b) Slow down so that your vehicle is exactly 28.77655 (recurring) metres from the angle of incidence between your left wing mirror and the next but one car's aerial.

c) Use your Exocet missiles to clear the road ahead.

d) Slow down so that your vehicle is exactly 28.7655 (recurring) metres from the angle of incidence between your left wing mirror and the next but one car's aerial.

30 You are towing a caravan. You should: **SELECT TWO ANSWERS**

a) Ask yourself how it could have come to this.

b) Stop and pull over whenever a vehicle is forced to slow down behind you out of a sense of personal shame.

c) Not allow yourself to get excited by things like awnings.

d) Probably have an affair.

Vehicle handling

31 Under what circumstances is it permitted to be stationary on a box junction? **SELECT FOUR ANSWERS**

a) When my vehicle has stopped moving and I have boxes on board.

b) When I am driving a White Van and people expect it of me.

c) When none of my wheels are in contact with any of the yellow markings.

d) When it turns out I haven't read the rest of this book – or any book, for that matter.

32 Why must you reduce your speed when driving in snow? **SELECT ONE ANSWER**

a) Because everything is so pretty.

b) Because it's Christmas and Jesus says so.

c) Because the gritter lorry in front of you is about to break down.

d) Because if I say I will, I stand more chance of passing this theory test and all you bureaufascists will let me out onto the roads.

33 To keep alert while driving at night you should not: **SELECT FIVE ANSWERS**
☐ **a)** Make yourself a nice cup of warm milky Horlicks.
☐ **b)** Listen to Radio 2.
☐ **c)** Toke from the bottle of anaesthetic gas you skilfully stole from the hospital when you were discharged after your last road accident.
☐ **d)** Attempt to drive while under a duvet.

34 Your brakes have suddenly become less effective. This is because: **SELECT ONE ANSWER**
☐ **a)** You are not driving and are merely stamping on the floor in front of the passenger seat.
☐ **b)** There is a small dog under the pedal, damping the action.
☐ **c)** Any one of a variety of technical problems, but that isn't important as you are just about to die.
☐ **d)** Your car is flying off a cliff.

35 You may not drive on a tramway unless: **SELECT ONE ANSWER**

☐ **a)** You drive a tram and you have the permission of the person who pays the electricity bill.
☐ **b)** You own a narrow-gauge Stannah stairlift that has been wired into your city's metro system and you have waited for the appropriate 'proceed' signal located behind the aspidistra by your front door.
☐ **c)** Your electric wheelchair is rated for 450 volts and has a bumper-car style power collection arm.
☐ **d)** You are a lonely man with an unfathomable passion for redundant transport infrastructure.

Motorway rules:

When joining a motorway you should be aware of: **SELECT TWO ANSWERS**
☐ NQDs stuck at the end of the slip road who are literally waiting for a written invitation to join the motorway.
☐ **b)** Remember the class system and straighten your tie and beg leave to join the motorway.
☐ **c)** Watch out for White Vans and give them plenty of room.
☐ **d)** Your own mortality.
Which **TWO** of these vehicles are not allowed to join a motorway:

■ Horse and cart.
- **b)** Lorry.
- **c)** Lorry full of horse and carts.
- **d)** Cart full of horses and lorries.

You are driving on a motorway. A lorry carrying a flammable load jackknifes in front of you. You should: **SELECT TWO ANSWERS**
- **a)** Check you are wearing clean underpants.
- **b)** Perform a handbrake turn and drive back the way you came along the hard shoulder.
- **c)** Marvel at what being so close to an explosion feels like.
- **d)** Listen out for the swoosh of the scythe.

A White Van pulls up along your left-hand side and the driver smiles at you in a sinister way. You should: **SELECT ONE ANSWER**
- **a)** Hold up a white flag and vacate the motorway at the next available exit.
- **b)** Accelerate and give him the finger.
- **c)** Cry.
- **d)** Empty your bowels.

You are driving along a motorway when 'Sususudio' by Phil Collins comes on the radio. You should: **SELECT ONE ANSWER**
- **a)** Tap your fingers on your steering wheel and remember how popular he was in the Eighties when he even cared about homeless people and everything.
- **b)** Suddenly develop empathy for people so depressed they would gladly remove their own eyes with a sharpened spoon just to give their lives a hint of variety and meaning.

- **c)** Turn your radio off immediately in case you are overcome with misery and feel compelled to drive to your death over the next bridge.
- **d)** Turn it up and sing along to your mother's corpse you've been driving around the M25 with in the passenger seat for the last seventeen hours.

Rules of the road

41 Do you know the special rules that apply to yellow box junctions? **SELECT ONE ANSWER**
- ☐ **a)** No, but if you hum the first few bars, I'll pick it up and join in later.
- ☐ **b)** You may only turn right into the path of speeding heavy goods vehicles.
- ☐ **c)** You may only use it as a hopscotch pitch at the weekend.
- ☐ **d)** All rules are the fascistic construct of the ruling elite.

42 How can you tell that a train is approaching at a level crossing? **SELECT ONE ANSWER**
- ☐ **a)** By listening to the announcements at the adjacent station.
- ☐ **b)** By careful observation of the train bearing down on you as you feverishly attempt to restart the car.
- ☐ **c)** By noting which set of tracks the evil genius has tied the heroine to.
- ☐ **d)** By perusing the relevant train operating company's timetable and adding eighty-five minutes to the stated times.

43 You are towing a caravan on a single-carriageway road. What must you never do? **SELECT ONE ANSWER**
- ☐ **a)** Reproduce, on the off-chance that you will blight your offspring with the same latent conehead scout leader tendencies you are clearly cursed with.
- ☐ **b)** Go postal in a layby with the jockey wheel.
- ☐ **c)** Fill the caravan with anthrax, in case of an accident.
- ☐ **d)** Need we go on? You get the picture, surely.

44 To keep your vehicle safe at night, you should: **SELECT CORRECT ANSWER**
- ☐ **a)** Park it outside your house with a chain leading in through your letterbox and attached to your toilet cistern. This makes a cheap, but reliable alarm system – you will be alerted to the theft of your car by the destruction of your front door and the flooding of your bathroom.
- ☐ **b)** Crash it through the front wall of a police station.
- ☐ **c)** Buy a really joyless, shitty vehicle.
- ☐ **d)** Resist the urge to have it stolen in order to claim the insurance so often.

45 Which of the following is authorized to stop you in your vehicle? **SELECT ALL ANSWERS**

☐ **a)** TV licence detector van.

☐ **b)** High Court judge wearing a redhead wig.

☐ **c)** Any bored police officer.

☐ **d)** Parking attendant with ideas above their station.

Road signs and markings

46 What is the purpose of the following road markings? **SELECT ONE ANSWER**

☐ **a)** The white line painters at the local council are all having nervous breakdowns and will be sent home to chevron their lounges.

☐ **b)** It is part of an intergalactic match in a sophisticated Tetris-like game and we are all the unwitting pawns of a higher civilization.

☐ **c)** A TV prank show has come up with a ridiculously unsafe method of getting people across the road, based as it is on principles of courtesy, patience and other medieval notions.

☐ **d)** I find, as I get older, very few things have any real purpose at all.

47 This sign indicates a steep section of road on a hill, but what does the percentage figure represent? **SELECT ONE ANSWER**

☐ **a)** Your chances of reaching the bottom alive.

☐ **b)** The hill's score on the TV clip show *I Love the 100 Most Interesting Hills from the 1970s*.

☐ **c)** Your clapped-out car's chances of reaching the top of the hill.

☐ **d)** The odds-on favourite's starting price for tomorrow's 4.30 at Haydock Park.

48 Which type of sign tells you to not do something? **SELECT ONE ANSWER**

☐ a)

☐ b)

NO
DON'T
UTTERLY
NOT

☐ c)

☐ d)

49 In the hangmanogram below, can you find out who the parking space is reserved for before you are hanged? **SELECT ONE ANSWER OR DIE**

☐ **a)** Kerb crawler.

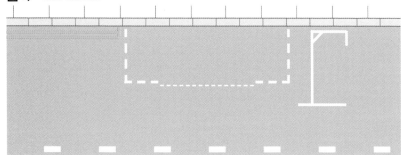

☐ **b)** Information architect. You need to know where anyone parks who describes themselves, without the faintest scrap of irony, as an information architect. You need to know so that you can visit their car daily and snap their wing mirrors off.

☐ **c)** Doctor of Philosophy.

☐ **d)** Dentist of truth.

50 What are these road markings for? **SELECT ONE ANSWER**

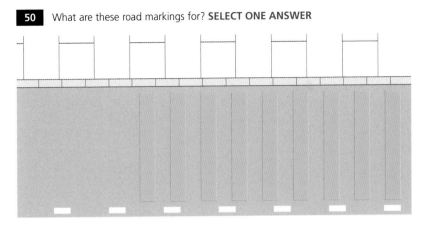

☐ **a)** To alert drivers to the dangers of wasps and bees entering the vehicle.

☐ **b)** To induce mental seizures on the approach to a major junction by mimicking the theta-wave pulse of the cerebral cortex.

☐ **c)** To use up some paint.

☐ **d)** To make the road seem jollier.

Congratulations

You have completed your theory test. Please put your pen down, but do not close this book until you have finished reading it.

No turning
back

P cont.

Q

R

S

T

traffic lights 34, 53, 90, 91
traffic wardens 33
traffic-calming 44
trams 88–89

U

Übermenschian forcefield 22
unwanted wheelchairs 3

V

vacuum-cleaner salesperson,
    moral complexity of 9
valkyries, ride of the 116
Volvo 94

W

warning signs 97–98
weather 60
wet room public convenience 78
wheelies 28
wheels 30
White Van Man 120, 121
White Van Man Arm 60
wickerwork workshops 2
Wimbledon junctions 112

Z

Zebra crossings 10
Zebra crossings, evil twin 10
Zimmer frames 3

About the 'authors'

Dan Kieran

Dan Kieran was the editor of the original bestselling 'Crap' trilogy: *Crap Towns I & II, Crap Jobs* and *Crap Holidays*. He is Deputy Editor of *the Idler* magazine and has been published in *The Times, Daily Telegraph, Guardian, Observer* and *Sunday Times Travel Magazine*. His next book, *I Fought the Law – A quest to break the stangest laws in Britain*, comes out in March 2007.

Dan passed his driving test, with only two minor faults, in September 2005. He lives in London with his fiancée Rachel and their son Wilf.

Ian Vince

Ian Vince was born in Brighton in 1964 and has lived almost everywhere – from East Anglia to the West Country – ever since. In 2004 he moved from deepest Cornwall to central London in a successful attempt to turn his life upside-down.

Since arriving in London, he has created the award-winning Department of Social Scrutiny website at www.socialscrutiny.org, as well as its satire format tie-in book, *Britain: What A State* (Boxtree, 2005). He has also contributed to a number of print and broadcast ventures including those of *Vera Productions, Zeppotron Productions* and *the Idler* magazine of which he is now a contributing editor. He is currently writing yet more books, articles and a narrative TV sketch show.

An evolutionary road safety adaptation in Ian's brain ensures that, if he were ever allowed to drive, he would be too vague to find his car keys. He lives in London with his wife, Kate.

Acknowledgements

Dan and Ian would like to thank the following for their help, assistance and enthusiasm.

Richard Milner with his accelerating office chair and Dusty Miller at Boxtree. Simon and Jo at MayerBenham. James Poulton, Gareth Kieran, Rob Vince, Rob Oaten, Kevin Parr, Lawrence Pointer, Clare Pollard, Will Hogan and all our long-suffering families and friends.

Picture credits

Isometric and overhead images of cars are taken from the authors' own photographs. All road layouts and most signs and signals were constructed by digital means.

All other images in *The Myway Code* have been supplied by www.absolutvision.com, the Jupiter Images Corporation website www.clipart.com and public domain images from the *Open Clip Art Library* at www.openclipart.org